A Soulful Guide to Embracing Restlessness,
Reframing Creative Unease, and
Finding Beauty in the Unfinished

THE JOY OF DISCONTENT

DAVID S. MORGAN

A Note Before We Begin

This is not a book of quick fixes or five-step plans.

It's a companion for those who feel the quiet ache of "not quite there yet"—even when life looks good from the outside.

You might be an artist or entrepreneur, a teacher or parent, a leader or seeker—or simply someone who feels the hum beneath the surface, that restless pull toward something more honest, more whole, more alive.

This book isn't here to quiet that restlessness. It's here to honor it.

Each chapter begins with a short poem—an opening gesture rather than a summary. You'll find stories, research, and reflective practices woven throughout, but always in service of something deeper than information: transformation—through restlessness, creative reframing, and the joy of being beautifully unfinished.

If you've grown weary of arrival myths and hollow milestones, if you're ready to explore a creative life shaped more by presence than by perfection, you're in the right place.

Let's begin with the ache.

Table of Contents

A Note Before We Begin ii

Introduction v

Chapter 1: The Myth of Arrival 1

    The Mirage of Arrival 2

    The Problem With "Done" 4

    Creating from the Middle 6

    A New Definition of Success 8

Chapter 2: Restlessness as a Creative Compass 13

    The Compass Within 14

    The Creative Urge Beneath Discontent 17

    Curiosity: The Engine of Becoming 19

    A Practice: Following the Twitch 22

Chapter 3: The Friction That Fuels Flow 29

    Flow Isn't Effortless—It's Engaged 30

    Neuroscience at the Edge 32

    Why We Resist What We Need 33

    The Joy in the Friction 44

Chapter 4: Creating Without Clinging 47

    The Art of Letting Go 48

THE JOY OF DISCONTENT

Eastern Wisdom Meets Everyday Practice 50

Why Outcome Obsession Kills Joy 55

The World Doesn't Need Perfect. It Needs Real. 64

Chapter 5: Joy as Rebellion 71

The Radical Act of Caring 72

Discontent as the Spark of Change 74

Choosing Joy When It's Easier Not To 82

Rebellion Through Beauty 85

Chapter 6: The Beautiful Unfinished 95

The Pirahã and the Language of Now 96

Completion Is a Concept. Creation Is a State. 98

Becoming Is a Lifelong State 105

Incompletion Isn't Inadequacy— 108

Chapter 7: In Practice — Honoring What Stirs 119

A Creative Companion 120

Practices to Return To 124

A Final Reflection— Stay Restless, Stay True 128

Acknowledgments 139

Suggested Reading & Inspirations 141

About the Author 142

Other Books by David S. Morgan 143

Notes 144

Introduction

The Quiet Fire: On the Beauty of Restlessness

There's a kind of discontent that doesn't scream.

It doesn't rage or wallow.

It hums—just under the surface.

A whisper that says: *This isn't quite it.*

Not yet.

It arrives in the spaces between accomplishments. In the quiet after the applause fades. In the morning light when you wake and feel that familiar tug—that sense that something remains unfinished within you.

It's easy to mistake that feeling for failure. Or impatience. Or not being grateful enough for what you have.

But what if that ache—that unshakable sense that more is possible—isn't a flaw at all?

What if it's the beginning of something beautiful?

This book is about the *joy* that lives inside that restlessness.

Not the joy of finishing something, or achieving something, or getting it "right."

But the deeper, wilder joy of *engaging*—of being pulled into something because your heart knows it matters.

The Joy of Discontent

Even when it's messy.

Especially when it's messy.

This isn't just for artists, entrepreneurs, or those who identify as "creatives." This is for anyone who feels the ache of wanting more than survival—the teacher reshaping her classroom against standardized expectations, the nurse who redesigns a patient care protocol, the factory worker who finds dignity in small improvements to his station, the parent who reinvents family traditions to reflect deeper values. This is for all who sense that quiet fire within, even if they've never had a name for it.

The Paradox of Creative Tension

We live in a world obsessed with outcomes. Metrics. Milestones. Mastery.

Our culture celebrates arrival, completion, the clean edges of certainty.

But creation is rarely clean or linear. It's often born in friction. In longing.

In a moment of quiet rebellion where you say:

This isn't enough. And I care too much to let it stay this way.

That is discontent.

But not the bitter kind.

The generative kind.

The kind that makes artists pick up the brush again.

That makes builders keep revising.

That makes the restless soul step forward when it would be easier to stay still.

Introduction

I think of Rosa, a school cafeteria worker I met while researching this book. For twenty years, she served meals within a system designed for efficiency, not connection. But something in her couldn't accept the assembly-line feeling of her work. So she began learning students' names. Developed a system of notes with small encouragements. Created a dignified dining space with plants she tended herself. "I couldn't change the menu," she told me, "but I could change the feeling of the room." Her discontent wasn't bitterness—it was the seed of transformation.

I've spent years studying this kind of creative tension—both in my own work and in the lives of makers, leaders, and everyday visionaries who create not in spite of discomfort, but because of it. What I've discovered is this: the most vibrant, alive people I know aren't those who have eliminated struggle. They're the ones who have found meaning within it.

Beyond Toxic Positivity

This is not a book about positive thinking. It's not about ignoring what's broken or pretending everything is fine.

It's about something more honest: the recognition that discomfort—when approached with curiosity rather than fear—can become a doorway. A compass. A creative spark.

I've come to believe this kind of discontent isn't something we should fix or flee.

It's something we can *honor*.

And when we do—when we stay present with the ache instead of numbing it—we find ourselves in the most sacred of human places:

The act of making. Of becoming. Of caring enough to create something that didn't exist before.

A Different Path

Our conventional wisdom says: Find contentment. Seek peace. Arrive.

This book proposes something different: What if the greatest joy isn't in arrival, but in movement? Not in certainty, but in curiosity? Not in having finished, but in forever becoming?

What if the ache of "not there yet" isn't something to overcome, but something to befriend?

Through stories, research, and reflective practices, we'll explore how creative discontent can become:

- A compass that guides us toward meaningful work
- A threshold that opens into flow
- A practice of creating without clinging to outcomes
- A form of quiet rebellion against apathy
- A celebration of the beautifully unfinished life

For the Restless Hearts

This is not a book of answers.

It's a companion for the creative path.

For those who feel something stirring, even if they can't name it yet.

For those who are tired of chasing "success" but still feel called to build, to write, to lead, to shape.

For those who believe that being unfinished doesn't mean you're broken. It means you're still *becoming*.

There is joy in that.

There is joy in you.

Even—especially—in your discontent.

INTRODUCTION

We begin, not with the answers, but with the ache. The quiet pull that says, There's more than this. In the next chapter, we'll explore why so many of us wait for the finish line—and what happens when we realize there may not be one.

Let's begin.

The Joy of Discontent

CHAPTER 1

The Myth of Arrival

> **Destination**
> *We dreamed of a finish line,*
> *painted gold and glowing.*
> *But the path kept moving—*
> *not to mock us,*
> *but to invite us*
> *to keep becoming.*
> *We've been sold a promise.*

It's subtle, woven into the culture like stitching you can't quite see unless you tug on the seam. The promise goes something like this: *Work hard, check the boxes, do the right things...* and one day, you'll arrive.

You'll reach a moment of completion.

Certainty.

Peace.

Arrival.

But what if that promise is a myth?

What if that moment doesn't exist—not because we're doing it wrong, but because we're wired for something else entirely?

In this book, I sometimes use "discomfort" and "discontent" interchangeably—not because they're the same, but because they often arrive together. Discomfort is the hum beneath the surface—the bodily tug that something's off. Discontent is the name we start to give that tug when we begin to listen. One stirs the body, the other shapes the story. Together, they form the soil of creative transformation.

THE MIRAGE OF ARRIVAL

Our world loves tidy endings. We measure lives in achievements, milestones, and arrivals:

- The diploma on the wall.
- The title on the business card.
- The house with the white picket fence.
- The book deal, finally signed.
- The next "next" that promises fulfillment.

Each one dangled like a carrot just beyond the moment we're in. We chase them with determination, believing that once we reach them, something will fundamentally shift. We'll feel complete. Satisfied. We will have *arrived*.

But so many of us have felt it—that strange emptiness after we've checked the box. The relief is real, but fleeting. The longing returns. Sometimes stronger than before.

I remember standing at my own book launch not so long ago, champagne in hand, surrounded by well-wishers. It was the moment I'd worked toward for nearly a decade. And yet, beneath the genuine gratitude, I felt a curious hollowness. Not depression or disappointment exactly—but a quiet question: *Is this it?*

It wasn't ingratitude. It was my creative self already stirring, already sensing that arrival isn't a destination. It's a threshold. Another beginning.

This mirage of arrival permeates our cultural narrative. Our films end with the triumphant victory, the wedding, the ride into the sunset. Our stories rarely show what happens next—the new challenges that emerge, the next mountain that appears on the horizon.

The novelist Toni Morrison captured this perfectly when she described her experience after winning the Nobel Prize for Literature: "It was a very isolated, lovely, flattering, but isolating experience," she said. "I don't know at what point one might say, 'Now I can relax'... but I don't think it has anything to do with having done something."

Even at the pinnacle of recognition, the feeling of having "made it" remained elusive.

This feeling isn't limited to creative achievement. I've spoken with CEOs who finally reached the corner office only to discover it wasn't what they imagined. With parents who raised their children perfectly, only to feel a void when they left home. With athletes who won the championship but found themselves asking, "What now?"

The pattern is remarkably consistent: achievement brings momentary joy, but rarely the sustained satisfaction we expect.

This fixation on arrival and individual achievement isn't universal. Many cultures around the world measure success through different lenses entirely. In Japanese philosophy, there's the concept of "kaizen" or continuous improvement, which values the ongoing process over any final state. Many Indigenous communities measure achievement through contribution to collective harmony and generational impact rather than personal milestones. In parts of Scandinavia, the concept of "lagom" (meaning "just enough") challenges the very idea that more achievement equals more fulfillment. These alternative perspectives remind us that our relentless pursuit of arrival points might be culturally conditioned rather than an inherent human need.

What makes this mirage so powerful? Part of it lies in our neurobiology. Our brains are wired to pursue, to seek, to strive. Dopamine, often called the "reward neurotransmitter," actually spikes in anticipation of reward—not in receiving it. We're literally designed to want more than we have.

But culture amplifies this natural tendency. From childhood, we're conditioned to organize our lives around endpoints: the good grade, the college acceptance, the promotion, the retirement plan. Even our leisure becomes achievement-oriented: the vacation we document to prove we were there, the hobby we master rather than simply enjoy.

The irony is painful: in our relentless pursuit of arrival, we miss the journey entirely. We treat the present as merely a means to a future state, never realizing that the present is all we ever have.

This can feel disorienting at first—like the ground keeps shifting under your feet. But if we look deeper, there's a quiet beauty in the motion. The sense that we are not done. That something within us still wants to grow, create, expand.

That is where joy hides—not in arrival, but in engagement.

The Problem With "Done"

The myth of arrival isn't just false—it's actively damaging. It trains us to see the journey as a means to an end. To push through the discomfort, the uncertainty, the mess—just to get to the other side.

But what if the mess *is* the magic?

What if the stumbling, the shaping, the refining—*is the point?*

The psychologist Mihaly Csikszentmihalyi, who pioneered the concept of "flow," found something surprising in his decades of research: people report their deepest satisfaction not when they're relaxing on vacation or celebrating a win, but when they're fully absorbed in meaningful challenge.

In other words: we're happiest not when we've arrived, but when we're engaged in becoming.

This insight runs counter to everything our achievement-oriented culture tells us. We're taught to endure the journey to reach the destination. To tolerate the process for the sake of the product. To sacrifice now for reward later.

But what if this equation is backward?

Consider the craftsperson who spends decades perfecting their skill. Yes, they create beautiful objects—but ask them about their work, and they'll tell you about the process. The particular way the material feels under their hands. The subtle decisions they make with each piece. The ongoing conversation between maker and made.

Their joy doesn't come from finishing the project. It comes from being fully immersed in the making.

The same is true for the scientist pursuing a question, the parent raising a child, the gardener tending plants, the athlete improving their form. In each case, the moments of deepest satisfaction come not from completion, but from engagement—from being fully present to the unfolding process.

When we fixate on the destination, we numb the experience of becoming. We miss the subtle shifts, the breakthroughs born from tension, the moments of awe that don't make it into our highlight reels.

This fixation on "done" also breeds a peculiar kind of anxiety. If our worth is tied to completion, then our unfinished projects become indictments. Our unreached goals become evidence of failure. Our ongoing questions become signs of inadequacy.

We begin to live in a perpetual state of "not enough yet"—always striving, never arriving.

The education system reinforces this mindset. Students learn to see assignments as hurdles to clear rather than opportunities to explore. The question becomes "Did I finish?" rather than "What did I discover?" The focus shifts from learning to completion.

Even our approach to personal growth falls prey to this thinking. We try to "fix" ourselves, to become "better versions" as if we're products to be perfected rather than living beings in constant evolution.

What might change if we valued process over completion? If we saw the unfinished, the imperfect, the in-process as not just acceptable but beautiful?

Joy is not a fixed place on a map. It's a current. A way of moving through the world.

CREATING FROM THE MIDDLE

So where does this leave us?

It leaves us here.

In the middle.

In the place where we don't yet know the ending.

Where we're still shaping, questioning, unfolding.

And that is a sacred place to be.

It is here—in this space of uncertainty and desire—that our creative self wakes up. That part of us that doesn't need to arrive, because it knows the joy is in the making.

Creating from the middle means embracing the generative power of the uncertain. It means recognizing that life—real, vibrant, meaningful life—happens not in the endings, but in the midst.

Consider the jazz musician improvising. She doesn't know exactly where the music will go. She begins with a theme, perhaps, but then she listens. Responds. Follows the emerging sound. Her art exists precisely because she's willing to create from the middle—to make without knowing the end.

Or think of the conversation that changes your perspective. It doesn't follow a script. It unfolds through question and response, through the willingness of both parties to enter uncertain terrain, to speak without knowing exactly what they'll say, to listen without knowing what they'll hear.

The middle is where discovery happens. Where surprise enters. Where we encounter both our limits and our unexpected capacities.

But creating from the middle isn't just about art or conversation. It's about how we approach every dimension of our lives.

It's the entrepreneur who launches before everything is perfect, who stays responsive to what emerges.

It's the parent who recognizes that raising children isn't about producing a particular "outcome," but about being present to the unfolding relationship.

It's the community that addresses complex problems not with rigid five-year plans, but with iterative approaches that evolve as understanding deepens.

To live creatively isn't about being an artist in the traditional sense. It's about engaging with life as a canvas. Responding. Inventing. Caring.

You can live creatively in a factory, in a kitchen, in a nonprofit, in the way you parent, in the way you lead.

And you don't need to wait for permission.

Creating from the middle requires a particular kind of courage. Not the courage to push through to the finish line, but the courage to remain in the uncertainty. To trust the process. To believe that meaning emerges not just from completion, but from engagement.

It's the courage to say: I don't know exactly where this is going. But I'm committed to the exploration.

This stance toward life opens us to joy in a way that arrival-thinking cannot. When we're not fixated on endpoints, we become available to the moment. We notice more. We respond more freely. We discover possibilities that wouldn't appear if we were charging straight toward a predetermined destination.

The middle isn't something to endure. It's something to inhabit.

A New Definition of Success

What if we redefined success?

Not as arrival.

Not as mastery.

But as *motion* toward what matters.

Success, then, becomes the act of aligning your life with what you care about—even if it's incomplete. Even if it's messy. Even if no one else sees it.

There's something beautifully rebellious in saying:

- I will keep going.
- I will keep making.
- I will keep becoming.

Not because I'm not enough.

But because I am deeply alive.

This redefinition asks us to shift our metrics. Instead of measuring outcomes, we measure alignment. Instead of asking "Did I arrive?" we ask "Am I moving in a direction that matters to me?"

The poet David Whyte captures this perfectly when he writes: "The antidote to exhaustion is not rest. The antidote to exhaustion is wholeheartedness."

Wholeheartedness isn't arrival. It's presence. It's care. It's the willingness to be where we are, feel what we feel, and respond with our full creative capacity.

This definition of success liberates us from the tyranny of comparison. When success is arrival, we're constantly measuring our progress against others. When success is alignment, we turn inward to our own compass.

It also frees us from the paralysis of perfectionism. When success is defined by flawless outcomes, we hesitate to begin. When success is alignment, we can start messy. We can embrace the stumbling steps. We can trust that the path emerges through walking, not before.

This reframing changes how we approach legacy, too. Legacy becomes not what we leave behind—the static artifacts of our accomplishments—but the quality of motion we bring to each day. The care with which we engage. The aliveness we cultivate and share.

Maria, a client of mine, spent fifteen years climbing the corporate ladder. She did everything "right"—advanced degrees, strategic career moves, sacrifices of time and energy. When she finally landed the C-suite position she'd been targeting, she gave herself two weeks to celebrate. Then she'd get down to enjoying her arrival.

Two months later, she called me.

"I thought I'd feel different," she said. "I thought I'd finally feel... I don't know. Complete?"

Instead, she felt restless. Not because the job wasn't good—it was challenging work she genuinely cared about. But because she'd been operating on the assumption that this achievement would somehow transform her inner landscape. That arrival would quench the very hunger that had driven her to excel.

It didn't.

Over the following year, Maria gradually shifted her definition of success. Rather than focusing on the next rung of the ladder, she began asking what kind of leader she wanted to be today. How she wanted to show up for her team, her organization, herself.

She didn't become less driven or ambitious. But her ambition changed character. It became less about reaching endpoints and more about embodying values. Less about arriving and more about engaging.

And paradoxically, this shift made her a more effective leader. Because she was no longer treating the present as a means to a future goal, she could be fully present to what was actually happening in her organization. She could listen more deeply, respond more creatively, lead more authentically.

Her story illustrates a profound truth: When we redefine success as alignment rather than arrival, we don't abandon achievement. We ground it in something more sustaining—the ongoing conversation between who we are and what we care about.

This is not a once-and-done shift. The pull of arrival-thinking runs deep in our culture and in our own conditioning. We'll still find ourselves fixating on endpoints, measuring our worth by outcomes, treating the present as merely a path to the future.

But each time we notice this pattern, we have a choice. We can gently bring ourselves back to the question of alignment. We can ask: What matters to me here? How can I move in that direction today? What would it mean to engage fully with what's before me?

Ultimately, this redefinition of success invites us to a more honest relationship with time. None of us knows how many days we have. To spend them perpetually reaching for future moments is to miss the one life we're given.

Success becomes the art of showing up fully for the life that's here. The one that's still unfolding. The one that never quite arrives, but is always becoming.

Reflection Practice: Honor Your Unfinished Symphony

Take some time with the following questions. There are no right answers—only your honest reflection.

1. **Audit your arrivals.** What are the "arrivals" you've been fixating on? Make a list of the endpoints you believe will bring you satisfaction, peace, or a sense of having "made it."

2. **Recall past arrivals.** Think of three significant achievements in your life—moments when you "arrived" at something you'd been working toward. How did each one feel in the days and weeks afterward? Did the satisfaction last? If not, what emerged in its place?
3. **Notice your middles.** Where in your life are you currently in "the middle" of something? A project, a relationship, a period of growth? How does it feel to be in this unfinished space?
4. **Feel your discontent.** Where do you feel a sense of creative restlessness? A pull toward something different or more aligned? What might this discomfort be trying to tell you?
5. **Imagine a shift.** What would change in your daily experience if you valued the middle as much as the endpoints? If you saw becoming as valuable as arriving?

Remember: Your worth doesn't depend on crossing finish lines. It lives in how fully you show up for the race itself.

If arrival is a myth, then what do we follow instead? What guides us forward when certainty fades? In the next chapter, we'll turn toward restlessness—not as a flaw, but as a compass.

The joy is in the becoming.

CHAPTER 2

Restlessness as a Creative Compass

The Itch
There is an itch beneath the calm,
a hum behind the quiet.
Not a flaw,
but a force.
Calling us to notice,
to reach,
to move.
We often try to quiet it.

That restless feeling that tugs at us while we sit still. That whisper that arrives when everything on paper seems fine—but something in us still stirs.

We call it discontent. Or distraction. Or anxiety.

But what if it's something else?

What if it's not a problem to fix, but a *signal to follow?*

The Compass Within

Restlessness has been misunderstood.

We've been taught to see it as a flaw—evidence of our inability to be grateful for what we have, proof of our culture's constant craving for more. When we feel that inner stirring, we're quick to judge it. To pathologize it. To see it as something to overcome.

What if we've been looking at it all wrong?

What if restlessness is not a bug in our system, but a feature? Not a problem to solve, but a sophisticated internal guidance mechanism pointing us toward growth, discovery, and creation?

Restlessness is not always about dissatisfaction with life—it's often a subtle call to *engage more deeply* with it. A kind of inner compass pointing toward what matters most. It's the pull that says, *"There's something here. Pay attention."*

Todd Kashdan, a psychologist who studies curiosity and psychological flexibility, describes this pull as an essential ingredient in meaning-making. He writes:

"Discomfort is the price of admission to a meaningful life."

His research reveals something counterintuitive: people who are willing to tolerate the tension of restlessness—rather than immediately seeking relief through distraction or easy comfort—report greater life satisfaction and sense of purpose over time.

This makes sense when we consider how innovation happens. Think of the most meaningful advances in human knowledge, art, or problem-solving. They rarely emerge from contentment with the status quo. They come from someone noticing what others overlook.

From feeling a friction that others ignore. From asking, "Could this be different?"

That friction is restlessness. And it's the beginning of creation.

Consider Grace Hopper, the computer scientist who pioneered machine-independent programming languages. When told that computers could only follow existing instructions, she felt a restlessness—a sense that there had to be a more intuitive way for humans and machines to communicate. That restlessness led her to develop the first compiler, fundamentally changing how we interact with computers.

Or think of Martha Graham, who felt confined by classical ballet's rigid structures. Rather than suppressing her discomfort, she followed it. She asked what a dance would look like if it emerged from the core of the body—from breath, contraction, release—rather than from preordained positions. Her restlessness gave birth to modern dance, reshaping the art form's possibilities.

These creators didn't achieve because they were free from restlessness. They achieved because they treated their restlessness as information. As a compass.

When we numb restlessness, we often numb potential.

When we listen to it, we begin to move—not away from ourselves, but toward something more aligned.

This isn't just true for artistic or scientific breakthroughs. It's equally relevant to the everyday creativity of living. The parent who feels something is off in their relationship with their teenager and initiates a difficult conversation. The teacher who notices students disengaging and redesigns the curriculum. The friend who senses unspoken tension and brings it to light.

The Joy of Discontent

Consider Elijah, a factory worker who'd operated the same machine for fifteen years. Day after day, the same motions, the same rhythm. The job paid well, and on paper, everything was fine. But a restlessness had been growing in him for months—a sense that something wasn't quite right with the workflow, that there was a better way to arrange his station.

At first, he tried to ignore it. Who was he to question the established system? But the discomfort persisted. Finally, one Tuesday morning, he arrived early and rearranged his workspace based on the intuitions that had been nagging him. He moved tools closer, adjusted the height of certain components, and created a simple tracking system for his materials.

The change seemed small, but the effect was profound. Not only did his efficiency improve, but a deeper satisfaction emerged in his work. His small creative response to restlessness revealed something important: even in highly structured environments, there is room for meaningful engagement, for bringing more of ourselves to what we do.

"I'd been treating restlessness as a sign I needed a new job," Elijah told me. "But it wasn't telling me to leave—it was telling me to engage differently with where I already was."

Each of these examples represents a response to restlessness—letting it guide toward more authentic engagement.

But following this compass requires courage. It means stepping into uncertainty. Risking failure. Facing resistance, both internal and external.

No wonder we often try to silence it.

Restlessness asks us to move when staying still would be easier. It invites us to speak when silence would be safer. It suggests that things could be different when acceptance would be more comfortable.

Yet, those who learn to trust this compass often discover something surprising: the discomfort of ignoring restlessness is ultimately greater than the discomfort of heeding it. There is a peculiar peace that comes not from quieting the call, but from responding to it—even if that response is messy and imperfect.

As Kashdan puts it, "The ability to be uncomfortable and continue to act with purpose is about as close to a superpower as humans get."

THE CREATIVE URGE BENEATH DISCONTENT

Have you ever felt oddly alive while reorganizing a space, drafting an idea you didn't fully understand yet, or sketching something just to see what it might become?

That's the creative self responding to the compass of restlessness.

It doesn't always start with clarity. It often starts with an itch—one you scratch not with answers, but with *action*.

We see this in artists and innovators, yes—but also in everyday creators:

- A teacher who rewrites the curriculum because the old one feels lifeless.
- A business owner who senses the culture has drifted from its purpose and begins reshaping it.
- A parent who, in the quiet of exhaustion, invents a new bedtime ritual that becomes sacred.

These are acts of response to the whisper: *"This could be better. This could be different. Let's see."*

The Joy of Discontent

Creativity, at its core, isn't about making art. It's about making meaning. It's about noticing what doesn't yet exist and bringing it into being. And that process almost always begins with a moment of discontent—a friction between what is and what could be.

The writer Ursula K. Le Guin captured this perfectly when she said: "The creative adult is the child who survived." She was pointing to the innate human capacity to respond to the world not just by accepting it, but by reimagining it.

Children do this naturally. Watch a child at play, and you'll see them constantly transforming their environment. The stick becomes a wand. The box becomes a fortress. They feel a creative urge, and they respond to it without hesitation or self-consciousness.

As adults, we often lose touch with this impulse. We become consumers rather than creators. We focus on fixing problems rather than exploring possibilities. We ask "What's wrong with me?" when we feel restless, rather than "What is this restlessness inviting me to create?"

But that creative urge doesn't disappear. It persists beneath the surface of our carefully ordered lives. And when we feel that inexplicable restlessness—that sense that something is missing or incomplete—it's often this creative self, nudging us to engage.

Consider the case of Maya, a corporate lawyer who spent years building a successful career. She had the title, the respect, the financial security. And yet, she felt a persistent restlessness she couldn't name.

"I thought something was wrong with me," she told me. "I had everything I was supposed to want."

But the restlessness persisted. It manifested as irritability, as difficulty sleeping, as a vague sense of disconnection from her work.

Rather than medicating these symptoms or dismissing them as ingratitude, Maya got curious. She started paying attention to when the restlessness intensified and when it quieted. She noticed it was loudest during certain types of cases and almost nonexistent when she was working on pro bono work with environmental causes.

This wasn't about hating her job. It was about her creative self recognizing a misalignment between her deepest values and how she was spending her days.

Maya didn't quit law. But she did begin redirecting her practice toward environmental law. She started writing about the intersection of corporate responsibility and sustainability. She initiated a green committee at her firm.

The restlessness didn't disappear—it transformed into creative energy.

"I realized I wasn't broken," she said. "I was being asked to create something that wasn't there yet."

This pattern plays out across domains. The restlessness that feels like a problem is often a creative urge looking for expression. The discontent that seems like a character flaw is often a compass pointing toward deeper alignment.

The question becomes not "How do I get rid of this feeling?" but "What is this feeling asking me to make, reshape, or bring into being?"

Curiosity: The Engine of Becoming

At the heart of this process is curiosity. Kashdan and others have shown that curiosity is not just a trait—it's a skill, a mindset, even a way of being.

And it's often triggered by restlessness.

The Joy of Discontent

Curiosity asks questions like:

- What's under this feeling?
- What would happen if...?
- What am I not seeing yet?

The difference between destructive discontent and generative restlessness lies in this shift—from frustration to *inquiry*.

Science fiction writer Octavia Butler captured this relationship with creative discontent through what she called "positive obsession." "Positive obsession is about not being able to stop just because you're afraid and full of doubts," she wrote (Butler, 1995).

For Butler, the creative twitch wasn't something to quiet, but something to follow with disciplined attention. "First forget inspiration. Habit is more dependable. Habit will sustain you whether you're inspired or not" (Butler, 1995).

What Butler understood was that creative restlessness isn't resolved through waiting for inspiration. It's answered through consistent engagement—through showing up for the work, day after day, regardless of how you feel. The twitch becomes not mere restlessness but an invitation to practice.

Curiosity transforms restlessness from a problem into a portal. It moves us from judgment to exploration, from stuckness to possibility.

Think of it this way: restlessness is the compass, pointing toward something that matters. Curiosity is the engine that propels us in that direction.

Research in neuroscience supports this. When we get curious about something, the brain releases dopamine—the same neurotransmitter associated with pleasure and motivation. Curiosity literally makes us feel good, encouraging us to keep exploring.

But even more fascinating is what curiosity does to our perception. Studies show that when we're curious, we actually see more. Our attention broadens. We notice details that would otherwise slip beneath our awareness. We make connections between disparate ideas.

This explains why some of the most significant breakthroughs in science, art, and business come not from focused problem-solving, but from open-ended curiosity. Alexander Fleming discovering penicillin by noticing the mold in his petri dishes. Pablo Picasso being influenced by African masks. Steve Jobs taking a calligraphy class that would later inform the design of the Macintosh.

In each case, curiosity allowed them to see beyond the obvious, to make connections across boundaries, to follow threads of interest without necessarily knowing where they would lead.

This kind of curiosity isn't just for geniuses or artists. It's available to all of us. It's the energy behind the gardener who experiments with new plant combinations, the cook who plays with unexpected flavors, the parent who discovers a fresh way to connect with their child.

Restlessness becomes joy when it opens into curiosity. When it invites us not to escape, but to explore.

But cultivating this curiosity requires a shift in how we relate to discomfort. Rather than seeing restlessness as something to fix, we learn to welcome it as the beginning of discovery. We get curious about our own experience.

This doesn't mean every moment of discontent leads to a major life change or creative breakthrough. Sometimes the exploration is subtle—a small adjustment, a new perspective, a moment of deeper understanding.

What matters is the stance: a willingness to turn toward restlessness rather than away from it. To ask "What's here?" instead of "How do I make this go away?"

As we develop this capacity, something remarkable happens. The restlessness itself begins to change character. It becomes less threatening, less overwhelming. We start to recognize it as a familiar ally in the creative process rather than an enemy to be vanquished.

We develop what psychologists call tolerance for ambiguity—the ability to remain open and engaged even when things are uncertain or unresolved. And this tolerance becomes a superpower in a world that's constantly changing, constantly presenting new challenges and opportunities.

Curiosity, it turns out, is not just the engine of becoming. It's the key to resilience in a world that never stops evolving.

A Practice: Following the Twitch

So, how do we actually work with restlessness as a creative compass? How do we cultivate the curiosity that transforms discontent into discovery?

It begins with a simple practice: noticing the twitch – a subtle embodied signal that something is pulling your attention.

In earlier drafts, I called it a flicker. But twitch feels truer—more visceral, more alive. A twitch is that small, nearly imperceptible jolt of attention, a bodily nudge toward something that matters. My next book, Flip the TWITCH, explores this idea in depth. But for now, know this: learning to notice and honor the twitch is the beginning of moving with purpose.

Try this:

Think of the last time you felt *off*. Not devastated—just unsettled.

Now pause. Ask:

- What wasn't aligned?
- What did I feel about the urge to tweak, shift, or move toward?
- What twitch was trying to get my attention?

That twitch may not have been calling you to start a company or write a novel. Maybe it just wanted you to walk a different route, change the tone of a conversation, or rearrange your desk.

Small restlessness can lead to big joy.

The key is learning to distinguish between different types of internal discomfort. Not all restlessness is creative in nature. Sometimes we're just tired. Or hungry. Or responding to external stress.

But creative restlessness has a particular quality. It's not just discomfort—it's discomfort with directional energy. It doesn't just want relief; it wants response. It has a vector, pointing toward something that matters.

Learning to recognize this specific flavor of restlessness takes practice. It's a subtle internal skill, like developing a palate for wine or an ear for music. But it's a skill worth cultivating, because it connects us directly to our creative capacity.

Here are some specific practices to develop this skill:

1. The Daily Check-In

Set aside five minutes each day to ask: "Where do I feel restless today? What is that restlessness asking of me?" Don't judge the answers. Just notice them. Over time, patterns will emerge.

2. The Creative Response

When you notice restlessness, respond with a small creative act. Write a paragraph. Sketch an image. Rearrange your space. Move your body in a new way. See what happens when you treat restlessness as an invitation to create rather than a problem to solve.

3. The Curiosity Walk

Take a walk with no destination. Follow what attracts your attention. Turn left when you feel pulled left. Stop when something interests you. Let curiosity be your guide. Notice how the restless mind often settles when the body is in motion.

4. The "What If" Game

When facing a challenge or feeling stuck, generate a list of "What if" questions. What if we approached this differently? What if the opposite were true? What if constraints were actually advantages? This playful inquiry can transform restlessness into possibility.

5. The Permission Slip

Write yourself a literal permission slip to explore something that calls to you, however impractical or uncertain it seems. "I give myself permission to..." This simple act can unlock creative energy that's been suppressed by practicality or fear.

These practices aren't about adding more to your to-do list. They're about developing a different relationship with the restlessness that's already there. About learning to see it not as an obstacle to peace, but as a doorway to deeper engagement.

As you work with these practices, you'll likely notice something surprising: following the flicker doesn't always lead where you expect.

Restlessness as a Creative Compass

It rarely follows a straight line. It may take you through detours and dead ends. It might ask you to backtrack or change direction entirely.

That's normal. The creative path isn't linear. It's exploratory. It's responsive. It unfolds as we engage with it.

The compass of restlessness doesn't always point to a specific destination. Sometimes it simply points toward the next step. The next question. The next possibility.

And that's enough. Because the joy isn't in arriving—it's in following the call. In answering yes to the creative urge beneath the discontent. In discovering what wants to emerge through you.

Restlessness as a form of care.

Discontent as a creative compass.

The itch as an invitation.

Not to escape the life you have, but to engage more deeply with the life that's calling.

Restlessness as a Form of Care

To be restless is to *care*.

To want more—for yourself, for others, for the work you do.

To be discontented with apathy or stagnation.

There is a quiet kind of love in the person who says:

"This could be better. Let's try."

That's the creative impulse.

That's the compass waking up.

In a world that often encourages us to settle, to adapt, to make peace with things as they are, there is something radical about honoring restlessness. It's a refusal to become numb. A commitment to staying awake to both the beauty and the brokenness of our world.

This kind of restlessness isn't about perfectionism. It's not about rejecting what is. It's about caring enough to imagine what could be.

It's the teacher who stays up late redesigning a lesson because they care about their students' engagement. The doctor who keeps researching because they care about finding better treatments. The citizen who shows up at community meetings because they care about their neighborhood's future.

This care-filled restlessness is at the heart of all meaningful change—both personal and collective.

Consider the civil rights movement. It began with a restlessness, a refusal to accept things as they were. But this restlessness wasn't just discontent. It was care—profound care for human dignity, for justice, for a world that more closely reflected deeper values.

Or think of the environmental movement. It started with people who couldn't rest easy with the degradation they witnessed. Their restlessness wasn't just anxiety about the future—it was care for the living world, for future generations, for the delicate balance that sustains us all.

Or perhaps Chris LeBrón, the Dominican singer who picked up a guitar in Bajos de Haina because something inside him stirred. That twitch led him from the backyard rehearsals to global collaborations—not because he knew where it would lead, but because he cared enough to follow the pull.

On a more personal scale, think of the parent who senses their child is struggling and can't just shrug it off. Their restlessness isn't neurosis—it's love, expressing itself as a refusal to ignore what matters.

Restlessness as a Creative Compass

When we frame restlessness as care, something shifts in how we relate to it. It's no longer something to suppress or overcome. It becomes something to honor—a sign that we're still engaged, still responsive, still alive to what matters.

This doesn't mean we act on every restless impulse. Not all forms of care require immediate action. Sometimes the most caring response is patience, or deep listening, or simply bearing witness.

But it does mean we stop pathologizing our own responsiveness to the world. We stop seeing our inability to just "be content" as a character flaw. We recognize it as the stirring of care—the movement of life continuing to unfold through us.

There's a beautiful term in the Jewish tradition: "tikkun olam." It means "repair of the world." It suggests that we are all participants in an ongoing process of healing and restoration. Our restlessness—our awareness of what remains broken or incomplete—is part of that process.

It's not a burden to be relieved of. It's a calling to be embraced.

So the next time you feel that stirring—that sense that something isn't quite right, that more is possible, that something wants to change—try framing it differently. Not as anxiety to be calmed, but as care asking to be expressed.

Ask yourself: What is this care for? What matters so much that I can't remain unmoved?

And then, with gentleness toward yourself and others, follow that care where it leads. Let it be your compass. Your engine. Your guide.

Because a world filled with people who care enough to feel restless—who refuse to become numb to either suffering or possibility—is a world that continues to evolve toward greater wholeness.

The Joy of Discontent

That, too, is the joy of discomfort. Not just the personal satisfaction of creative expression, but the deeper fulfillment of participating in the ongoing creation of a more beautiful world.

Once we begin listening to that twitch of discontent, something deeper starts to stir—an energy that wants to move. But movement isn't always ease. Sometimes, it starts in friction. Let's explore how that tension can lead us somewhere even more powerful: flow.

Restlessness as a form of care. Care as a form of love. Love as the ultimate creative force.

That's the compass within you. And it's always pointing home.

Pay attention to the twitch. It may be small, but it carries your next great question.

CHAPTER 3

The Friction That Fuels Flow

> ***Threshold***
> *Just before it opens,*
> *the door resists.*
> *Not to keep you out,*
> *but to make sure*
> *you're awake*
> *when you enter.*

There is a moment, just before immersion, when everything inside you wants to stop.

You sit before the canvas, the page, the problem—and feel a twitch of friction. Doubt. Resistance. The urge to walk away, check your phone, pour another cup of coffee.

But if you stay—just a little longer—you begin to move.

Something opens. Focus sharpens. Time thins. And suddenly, you're not trying anymore. You're *in it.*

This is the doorway to flow.

Flow Isn't Effortless—It's Engaged

We often speak of flow as if it's a magic state: graceful, natural, seamless. The athlete "in the zone." The musician lost in the music. The writer whose words seem to arrive from somewhere beyond conscious thought.

These moments appear effortless from the outside—as if the person has transcended struggle entirely. But this common perception misses something essential about flow.

Flow isn't the absence of effort—it's effort *transformed*.

Mihaly Csikszentmihalyi, the psychologist who pioneered the study of flow, defined it as "a state in which people are so involved in an activity that nothing else seems to matter; the experience is so enjoyable that people will continue to do it even at great cost, for the sheer sake of doing it."

What's striking about this definition is what it doesn't say. It doesn't describe flow as easy. It doesn't promise comfort. In fact, Csikszentmihalyi found that people are often happiest not when they're relaxing, but when they are *stretched*—engaged in meaningful challenge that demands their full capacity.

This is the paradox:

- Flow feels smooth, but it is born from friction.
- It looks effortless from the outside, but it demands full presence inside.

Consider the rock climber scaling a difficult route. From below, their movements might look fluid, even graceful. But ask the climber, and they'll tell you about the intense focus required, the constant micro-adjustments, the full engagement of body and mind.

Or think of the surgeon in the middle of a complex procedure. They may appear calm, their hands steady. But internally, they're completely absorbed—making countless decisions, drawing on years of training, responding moment by moment to what emerges.

What these experiences share isn't the absence of difficulty. It's the perfect match between challenge and capacity. The rock face is hard enough to demand full attention, but not so hard that it produces anxiety. The surgery requires complete focus, but not beyond what the surgeon is equipped to handle.

Csikszentmihalyi called this the "flow channel"—that sweet spot where we're operating at the edge of our abilities, fully engaged but not overwhelmed. Too little challenge, and we're bored. Too much, and we're anxious. But just right? That's where flow happens.

This insight transforms how we think about creative friction. The resistance we feel before flow—the doubt, the hesitation, the urge to distract ourselves—isn't an obstacle to be eliminated. It's a natural part of the process. It's the threshold we cross on our way to deeper engagement.

We don't get to flow by bypassing discomfort.

We get there by *leaning into* it.

The writer who pushes through the blank page eventually finds their rhythm. The musician who practices through the frustration reaches a moment when the music begins to flow. The athlete who works through fatigue discovers a second wind.

This is why flow isn't a passive state we simply fall into. It's an active engagement we cultivate through our willingness to stay with friction rather than flee from it.

As Csikszentmihalyi observed: "The best moments usually occur when a person's body or mind is stretched to its limits in a voluntary effort to accomplish something difficult and worthwhile."

The joy of flow isn't in escaping challenge.

It's in meeting it fully.

NEUROSCIENCE AT THE EDGE

What's happening in the brain during flow?

When we enter flow, several important shifts occur. The inner critic that usually narrates our experience—questioning, judging, monitoring—grows quieter. This happens as the prefrontal cortex, which manages self-reflection and self-criticism, temporarily steps back. Scientists call this "transient hypofrontality," and it's why flow feels like freedom from self-consciousness.

Meanwhile, the brain releases a powerful blend of neurochemicals. Dopamine sharpens focus and creates a sense of reward. Norepinephrine heightens attention. Endorphins generate pleasure and ease our perception of effort. The result is a state where we feel simultaneously energized and calm, challenged yet capable.

But here's the most important insight from neuroscience: this optimal brain state doesn't happen during comfort or routine. It happens at the edge—when we're pushing slightly beyond the familiar but not so far that we're overwhelmed.

Steven Kotler, who studies the neuroscience of flow, explains it simply: "Flow follows focus. It's maximized when attention is fully engaged in the present moment, and that happens most readily when we're pushing ourselves slightly beyond our comfort zone."

This explains why flow is often preceded by frustration or resistance. The brain doesn't activate this optimal state during easy, routine activities. It does so when we step up to a meaningful challenge—when we engage with the friction rather than avoid it.

Think of it as the brain's way of rising to the occasion. When we willingly take on meaningful challenge, powerful neurological mechanisms activate to help us meet it.

But the pathway isn't always smooth. There's often a dip before the rise—a period of struggle, frustration, or confusion that precedes the flow state. Researchers sometimes call this "the struggle phase," and it's a natural part of the process.

This neurological understanding offers a powerful reframe: the friction we feel before flow isn't a sign that something's wrong. It's a sign that we're at the edge—exactly where we need to be for flow to emerge.

And friction—our restlessness, our resistance—is often the signal that we're getting close.

Why We Resist What We Need

It's strange, isn't it?

We long for creative immersion, but avoid the tension that opens the door.

This is the great creative irony:

- We crave flow, but fear the threshold.
- We want depth, but seek distractions.

Why do we resist the very discomfort that leads to what we most desire?

Part of the answer lies in our evolutionary wiring. The human brain evolved in an environment where energy conservation was crucial for survival. Uncertainty and new challenges represented potential threats, consuming precious mental and physical resources.

Our default setting is efficiency—doing what we already know how to do, staying within familiar territory. This made perfect sense for our ancestors facing resource scarcity. It makes less sense in our world of abundant information and complex challenges that require creative engagement.

But our brains haven't caught up. They still follow ancient programming: conserve energy, avoid uncertainty, seek the known.

This programming manifests as resistance—that feeling of "I don't want to" that arises when we face the blank page, the difficult conversation, the new skill that hasn't yet become automatic. It shows up as procrastination, distraction, or sudden interest in reorganizing the spice rack when we sit down to write.

But there's another layer to this resistance. Flow requires vulnerability. To enter flow, we have to surrender conscious control, to trust a process we can't fully direct. We have to be willing to fail, to not know, to look foolish.

For many of us—especially those conditioned by education systems and workplaces that prize certainty and right answers—this vulnerability feels threatening. We've been trained to value control over surrender, knowing over exploring.

So we hesitate at the threshold. We feel the resistance and interpret it as a warning rather than an invitation.

Additionally, our digital environment constantly pulls us away from the depth that flow requires. Every notification, every new headline, every social media update creates what technology theorist Linda

Stone calls "continuous partial attention"—a state where we're always slightly distracted, never fully present.

Flow, by contrast, requires full presence. It demands that we temporarily step away from the stream of inputs and outputs to immerse deeply in one thing. That disengagement can feel uncomfortable in a culture that values constant connection and immediate response.

Given these powerful forces working against flow, it's no wonder we resist the threshold. But this resistance isn't a personal failing. It's a natural response to both our evolutionary programming and our cultural conditioning.

The resistance before flow is not a bug—it's the cost of admission.

And if we can reframe that friction not as a stop sign, but as a signal, everything changes.

You are not broken because it feels hard to start.

You are *on the threshold.*

Story: The Gardener's Flow

Rosa had been cooking dinner for her family every night for twenty years. What began as an act of necessity had gradually become a chore—one more task in her busy day, something to get through efficiently before moving on to the next responsibility.

But last spring, something shifted. Her daughter gave her a small raised garden bed as a birthday present. Reluctantly at first, Rosa began planting herbs and a few vegetables. She had no gardening experience and felt the familiar resistance to learning something new—that voice saying it was too complicated, too time-consuming, a distraction from her "real" responsibilities.

The Joy of Discontent

Still, she started. Small steps. Watering. Weeding. Watching.

One ordinary Wednesday evening, Rosa went to pick some basil for dinner. She knelt beside the garden, and as she reached for the fragrant leaves, something happened. Her attention fully engaged with the task—the scent of the herbs, the subtle variations in green, the way the plants had changed since yesterday. She noticed herself slowing down, fully present to this simple act of harvesting.

That evening's cooking transformed. No longer rushing to finish, she found herself absorbed in the process—the sizzle of garlic in oil, the changing colors of the vegetables, the choreography of moving between cutting board and stove. Time seemed to expand. Her senses sharpened.

"I've cooked thousands of meals," she told me later, "but that night I was actually *there* for it. I wasn't thinking about tomorrow's meeting or yesterday's argument. I was just... cooking."

What Rosa experienced wasn't some extraordinary achievement. It was flow in the midst of ordinary life—that state of full engagement that can happen not just on mountain peaks or concert stages, but in kitchens, gardens, workspaces, and conversations.

And like so many flow experiences, it began with friction—the initial resistance to starting something unfamiliar, the pull toward distraction, the subtle but persistent drive toward efficiency over presence.

"The garden changed how I cook," Rosa said. "Not because of the fresh ingredients, though those help. But because it taught me how to be there for the process. And that's where the joy was hiding all along."

The Maker's Shift

A friend of mine—a ceramicist—once told me she never knows if a day will be productive until her hands are covered in clay. "The resistance never leaves," she said. "But I've learned to start anyway. The friction fades."

Cecilia has been making pottery for over twenty years. Her pieces are in galleries and private collections. You might expect that by now, she would greet her work with easy confidence, sliding effortlessly into creative flow.

Yet nearly every morning, she feels the hesitation. The doubt. The pull toward easier activities. Sometimes she stands in her studio doorway for minutes, reluctant to begin.

What's striking isn't the art she makes—it's her *relationship* to the creative process.

She doesn't wait to feel inspired. She enters the discomfort. Touches the clay. Moves through the threshold.

"I used to think something was wrong with me," she told me. "All these years of practice, and I still face resistance. But then I noticed something: the resistance is just the beginning. It's not the whole story."

What she discovered was a pattern. The resistance was consistent, yes. But so was what followed when she stayed with it.

"There's this shift that happens. I can't predict exactly when—sometimes twenty minutes in, sometimes an hour. But almost without fail, I cross some invisible line. Suddenly, I'm not fighting anymore. I'm just... there. With the clay. In conversation with it."

This is the maker's shift—the transition from resistance to flow. It's not about eliminating the friction. It's about recognizing it as part of the journey rather than an obstacle to it.

Cecilia's experience isn't unique. Across domains, creators describe similar patterns. The composer who stares at blank staves before the melody comes. The writer who deletes a dozen false starts before finding the thread. The scientist who works through failed experiments before the breakthrough.

Within minutes, the resistance softens. Something deeper takes over.

That's flow.

Not mystical. Not magical. But *earned* through presence.

What these makers understand is that resistance isn't a sign to stop. It's a doorway to pass through. The feeling of "I don't want to" or "I don't know how" isn't the truth of our capacity—it's just the first message the brain sends when faced with a meaningful challenge.

If we listen only to that first message, we never discover what lies beyond it. If we retreat at the first sign of friction, we miss the deeper engagement waiting on the other side.

This doesn't mean forcing ourselves brutally through resistance. It means approaching it with curiosity rather than judgment. With patience rather than demand. With the understanding that this, too, is part of the creative process.

"Some days are harder than others," Cecilia admits. "Some days the shift takes longer. But knowing it's normal—that helps. Knowing I'm not broken or lazy or uncreative because I feel resistance—that's what allows me to keep showing up."

Her wisdom offers a powerful reframe for all of us who create, in whatever form: The obstacles aren't separate from the path. They are the path.

Resistance isn't the opposite of flow. It's often the *precondition*.

Friction in Other Forms

Flow isn't just for artists or athletes. It can show up:

- In a team solving a problem together.
- In a surgeon focused in the middle of a procedure.
- In a child building a tower until it stands.
- In a conversation that moves beyond small talk into genuine connection.
- In cooking a meal with full attention to the sensory experience.
- In a walk where you notice details that usually slip past awareness.

Anywhere there's full engagement, there's the potential for flow.

And always—*always*—there's friction first.

This universality matters because it reminds us that flow isn't reserved for special talents or extraordinary circumstances. It's a natural human capacity, available across domains and activities.

What triggers flow isn't the specific activity, but the quality of engagement we bring to it. The willingness to meet resistance, to stay present, to surrender to the process.

Consider teaching. At its best, teaching can be a profound flow experience. The teacher tunes into the room, responds to what emerges, adjusts in real time. They forget themselves in service to the students' learning.

But before that flow? There's the friction of preparation, of anticipating challenges, of managing anxiety about reaching every student. There's the resistance of starting the class, of engaging with uncertainty.

The teachers who find the most joy in their work aren't those who never feel this friction. They're the ones who recognize it as the threshold to deeper engagement.

Or think about parenting. Parents often experience flow in moments of deep connection with their children—playing together, sharing discoveries, navigating challenges as a team.

But these flow states are frequently preceded by the friction of exhaustion, of competing demands, of the effort required to be fully present when it would be easier to check out.

The parents who find flow aren't those who never feel resistance. They're those who gently move through it, trusting that connection waits on the other side.

Even in the workplace, often seen as the antithesis of flow, these dynamics apply. Knowledge workers report flow when tackling complex problems that stretch their abilities but still feel solvable. Surgeons experience flow during challenging procedures that demand their complete focus.

But before these states? The surgeon feels the weight of responsibility, the awareness of risk. The knowledge worker faces the blank document, the intimidating complexity of the problem.

The key is to recognize when resistance means *not now...* and when it means *lean in.*

Sometimes resistance truly is a signal to pause, to rest, to recalibrate. Not all friction leads to flow. But often, the friction we feel—the hesitation, the doubt, the urge to distract ourselves—is precisely the threshold we need to cross.

As we develop a more nuanced relationship with friction, we become better at distinguishing between these signals. We learn to recognize the particular quality of resistance that precedes flow—the resistance that isn't saying "stop," but rather "pay attention, something important is happening here."

We develop what Zen practitioners might call a "beginner's mind" toward resistance—approaching it with curiosity rather than assumption, with patience rather than demand.

Discontent isn't the opposite of flow. It's often the *precondition*.

The friction that seems to block our path often marks the entrance to the experience we seek.

Practices for Entering Flow

We can't force flow. But we can *set the stage*.

Flow emerges from a particular relationship between challenge and skill, between structure and surrender, between intention and attention. While we can't command it to appear, we can create conditions that make it more likely to visit.

Here are a few invitations to play with:

Narrow the focus. Flow thrives on clear boundaries. When attention is diffused across many targets, it lacks the concentration needed for flow. Before beginning a creative session, clarify what you're focusing on. Close unnecessary tabs. Put your phone in another room. Create a container for your attention.

As William James, the father of American psychology, observed: "The faculty of voluntarily bringing back a wandering attention, over and over again, is the very root of judgment, character, and will... An education which should improve this faculty would be the education par excellence."

This faculty—the ability to direct and hold attention—is precisely what creates the conditions for flow.

Honor the threshold. Expect resistance. Rather than being surprised or dismayed when it appears, recognize it as a natural part of the process. Say to yourself: "Ah, here's the threshold. I know this place." This simple acknowledgment can transform how you relate to creative friction.

The novelist Haruki Murakami described his approach this way: "The most important qualities for a novelist are probably persistence and endurance. I get up at 4 a.m. and work for five to six hours. In the afternoon, I run for 10 kilometers or swim for 1,500 meters, then I read a bit and listen to some music. I go to bed at 9 p.m. I keep to this routine every day."

Notice that Murakami doesn't wait for inspiration. He shows up consistently, honoring the process, moving through the threshold day after day.

Create a ritual. Rituals serve as bridges between ordinary consciousness and flow states. They signal to the mind and body that we're entering a different mode of engagement. Your ritual might be as simple as three deep breaths, or as elaborate as a specific sequence of preparations.

The key is consistency—doing the same thing each time you prepare to create. Over time, the ritual itself becomes a trigger for the mental state you're seeking.

Maya Angelou had a specific ritual for her writing: she would rent a hotel room, arrive at 6:30 a.m., and write until 2 p.m. She kept only a dictionary, a Bible, and a bottle of sherry in the room. This consistent structure created the conditions for her creativity to flow.

Stay long enough. Flow often doesn't begin until after the first false start. After the doubt, the hesitation, the critical thoughts. If you abandon ship at the first sign of turbulence, you'll never reach the smoother waters.

Give yourself a minimum time commitment. Twenty minutes. Thirty. An hour. Not with the demand that flow must appear in that time, but with the commitment to stay present to the process, whatever emerges.

As choreographer Twyla Tharp advises: "Ritual is about setting the time, and then showing up, no excuses. If you want to have creative flow in your life, you have to commit to a practice."

Let go of outcome. Flow thrives when we're *in it*, not when we're watching ourselves perform. The paradox of flow is that it arrives most readily when we're focused on the process rather than the product, on the experience rather than the evaluation.

This doesn't mean abandoning standards or goals. It means holding them lightly, letting them guide rather than govern the creative process.

Jazz musician Miles Davis captured this perfectly: "Do not fear mistakes. There are none." This stance—focused but not rigid, intentional but not controlling—creates the perfect conditions for flow.

Think of these practices as lighting a fire. You don't control the flame—but you can gather the kindling and strike the match.

The Joy in the Friction

Here's the real secret:

The joy isn't only *in* flow.

It's also in the *return to it.*

Each time you enter flow, you remember something about yourself.

That you are capable of full attention.

That you are built for deep focus.

That you are more than your distraction, more than your doubt.

This remembering is itself a profound joy. It's a homecoming to a state of being that feels fundamentally right—where you're neither drifting nor forcing, but engaged in a natural current of creativity.

Flow researcher Steven Kotler puts it this way: "Flow is the source code of intrinsic motivation." When we experience flow, we don't need external rewards to keep going. The activity becomes its own reward. We do it for the sheer joy of doing it.

This intrinsic motivation creates an upward spiral. We seek flow because it feels good, which leads us to engage in activities that create more flow, which strengthens our capacity for attention, which makes flow more accessible, and so on.

But here's the nuance that's often missed: The joy isn't just in the flow state itself. It's in the entire cycle—including the friction that precedes it and the integration that follows it.

The friction wakes us up. It asks us to choose: Will I disengage, or will I meet this moment? Will I retreat into comfort, or will I step toward aliveness?

The Friction That Fuels Flow

When we choose engagement—when we move toward the friction rather than away from it—we experience a particular kind of joy. Not the easy pleasure of comfort, but the deeper satisfaction of living at our edge. Of being fully in conversation with life rather than merely observing it.

This is the joy in the friction. The joy of choosing presence over escape, engagement over numbness. The joy of honoring the creative spark enough to stay with the process, even when it's uncomfortable.

Friction is a gift.

It wakes us up before we fall into the trance of comfort.

It reminds us that joy is waiting—not in ease, but in *engagement*.

And as we develop this relationship with friction—as we learn to see it not as an obstacle but as a threshold—something remarkable happens. We become more willing to step into uncertainty, to take creative risks, to engage with the edges of our capacity.

We develop what psychologists call "challenge tolerance"—the ability to stay steady in the face of difficulty rather than retreat from it. This capacity serves not just our creative pursuits, but our entire lives. It helps us navigate change, face difficult truths, and engage with the complex challenges of our world.

The ability to find joy in friction, to see discomfort as a doorway rather than a wall—this is perhaps the most valuable creative skill we can cultivate. It's what allows us to keep showing up, to keep creating, to keep growing in a world that constantly presents new challenges.

The flow state itself may be temporary, but the capacity to move through friction toward flow? That's a lifetime practice. And it's a practice that transforms not just what we create, but who we become in the process.

The Joy of Discontent

Flow teaches us to engage fully. But even in that engagement, the ego often lingers—asking, How will this be received? What will come of it? Next, we'll explore what happens when we create not for recognition, but for the joy of the act itself.

The joy is in the becoming. The friction is the invitation. The flow is the reminder of what's possible.

And together, they form the rhythm of a creative life.

CHAPTER 4

Creating Without Clinging

> *The Offering*
> *Make it,*
> *not to be praised,*
> *but to be poured out.*
> *Not to be kept,*
> *but to be given.*
> *A leaf on the river.*
> *A match in the dark.*

We live in a world that rewards the finished product.

Likes, shares, metrics, and milestones. External validation wrapped in digital applause.

But the creative act—the real one—isn't about that.

It's about engagement. Presence. The quiet joy of giving shape to what stirs within you.

And when we cling to outcomes—when we make only to be seen or celebrated—we lose the very soul of the thing we're trying to make.

THE JOY OF DISCONTENT

THE ART OF LETTING GO

To create without clinging is not to give up ambition or quality—it's to release the *need* for control over what happens after the making is done.

It's a deeply human paradox:

- We *care* deeply about what we make.
- But we find *freedom* when we detach from how it's received.

This paradox challenges our conventional understanding of creativity. We're taught that caring about outcomes motivates excellence. That attachment to results drives improvement. That concern for reception sharpens our work.

And there's some truth in this. Caring can indeed fuel commitment. But when caring hardens into clinging—into a desperate need for specific outcomes—something essential is lost. The work becomes rigid. Fearful. Calculated rather than authentic.

Consider the difference between these two creators:

The first labors over each detail, constantly imagining how the audience will receive it. Every choice is filtered through anticipated reaction. "Will they like this? Will this impress? Will this go viral?" The work becomes a vehicle for validation, a means to an end beyond itself.

The second cares just as deeply about quality, about precision, about the integrity of what they're making. But they hold their work differently. They ask not "How will this be received?" but "Is this true? Does this serve what wants to emerge? Is this aligned with what matters to me?" The work becomes an offering rather than a transaction.

Both may produce impressive results. But the experience of creating is vastly different. And often, paradoxically, the second creator's work resonates more deeply with others precisely because it wasn't shaped primarily for their approval.

This is the artist who writes a novel that no one may read, but does it anyway.

The founder who starts something from love, not just to scale.

The teacher who pours into a student, knowing they may never see the result.

These acts are offerings, not transactions.

But how do we actually practice this? How do we care deeply about our work without clinging to how it's received?

It begins with intention. Before starting a creative project, we can ask ourselves: "Why am I really doing this? What am I serving beyond my own need for validation?" This doesn't mean denying that we want recognition—that's natural. It means becoming clear about the deeper purpose that can sustain us when recognition doesn't come.

It continues with attention. As we create, we can notice when our focus shifts from the work itself to imagined outcomes. When we catch ourselves shaping the work for approval rather than authenticity, we can gently bring our attention back to the immediate creative conversation—to what the work itself is asking for.

And it culminates in release. When the work is done, we let it go. Not carelessly, but with the understanding that its journey is no longer ours to control. It will touch who it touches. It will mean what it means to those who encounter it. Our job is to create with integrity and then open our hands.

In 2005, Hayao Miyazaki offered a simple truth: "I don't make films with an audience in mind... I make them for myself, and if children like them, that's fine." It's a quiet rebellion against clinging—a reminder that joy lies not in who receives our work, but in the honest act of making it.

Notice the subtlety here. He cares deeply about his art—enough to pour his life into it. But he doesn't cling to how it's received. He creates authentically and then lets go.

This approach to creativity isn't just more joyful. It's often more effective. When we release the need for specific outcomes, we become more receptive to what actually wants to emerge in the work. We become more willing to take creative risks, to follow intuitive threads, to allow ourselves to be surprised by the process.

Paradoxically, by loosening our grip on the outcome, we often create work that's more likely to achieve the very recognition we're no longer desperate to receive.

EASTERN WISDOM MEETS EVERYDAY PRACTICE

This mindset isn't new—it echoes the wisdom of countless spiritual traditions. In the *Bhagavad Gita*, there is a powerful teaching:

"You have a right to your labor, but not to the fruits of your labor."

This idea—creating without attachment to results—isn't about apathy. It's about *liberation*. It frees us from ego, from fear, from the tyranny of expectation.

It invites us to show up, give our best, and let go.

Creating Without Clinging

For centuries, Eastern traditions like Buddhism and Taoism have seen the creative spark in non-attachment. The Zen concept of 'mushin' (無心) or 'no-mind' offers a presence so pure the self dissolves, letting action flow like breath—unfixed, unforced. This isn't indifference; it's a deep dive into the moment, free from the ego's restless chatter. The Taoist principle of 'wu wei' (無為) or 'non-doing' moves with the grain of things, rising gently to meet what calls, without strain or grasp. This isn't passivity; it's a quieter action, alive in the now, unshackled from the pull of what's next.

These ancient insights find surprising resonance in modern creativity research. Studies in creative cognition reveal that our most innovative ideas often emerge when we're less fixated on results and more open to unexpected connections. The psychological state called "cognitive flexibility"—our ability to adapt thinking and consider diverse perspectives—increases when we're not rigid about outcomes.

But how do we translate these Eastern concepts into everyday creative practice in our achievement-oriented Western context?

The key is to recognize that non-attachment doesn't mean not caring. It means caring in a way that doesn't constrict. It means pouring yourself fully into the creative act while releasing the need to control what happens next.

Consider the practice of improvisational music. Jazz musicians train rigorously in technique, in theory, in the traditions of their art form. They care deeply about their craft. But when they step on stage to improvise, they must simultaneously let go. They can't cling to pre-planned phrases or outcomes. They must be responsive to the moment, to what emerges in the interplay with other musicians.

This balance—between deep preparation and open responsiveness, between caring and releasing—is at the heart of creating without clinging.

Or think about scientific research. The most groundbreaking discoveries often come when scientists maintain methodical rigor while remaining open to unexpected findings. If they cling too tightly to their initial hypotheses or desired outcomes, they might miss the anomaly that leads to breakthrough.

As Louis Pasteur famously observed, "Chance favors the prepared mind." The prepared mind cares enough to do the work, to develop the skills, to show up consistently. But it doesn't cling so tightly to expected results that it misses what actually emerges.

This approach can transform not just artistic creation or scientific discovery, but everyday creative acts—from cooking a meal to facilitating a meeting, from writing an email to designing a garden.

In each case, we bring our full care and attention to the process. We prepare. We show up. We engage completely. And then we let go of controlling exactly how it unfolds or how it's received.

That doesn't mean we don't care about what matters.

It means we care enough to *not need control.*

The Choreographer's Surrender

Lena was used to applause.

As a choreographer for a regional dance company, she had built her career on precision—every movement rehearsed, every beat counted. Critics praised her exacting style, and audiences knew what to expect: tight, dazzling, controlled beauty.

But this piece was different.

Creating Without Clinging

It began as a tribute to her late sister, who had lived with schizophrenia. Lena wanted to capture the unpredictability, the broken rhythm, the fleeting clarity. But no matter how many drafts she sketched, something felt false—too polished. Too safe.

One rehearsal evening, a young dancer improvised a series of erratic, angular movements during a lull. It wasn't in the choreography—but it struck Lena like lightning.

It was raw. Uncomfortable. Alive.

She paused. Then did something she'd never done before: scrapped her planned choreography and asked the dancers to help her build a piece from improvisation. "Start with how you feel the rhythm shift," she told them. "We'll shape it together."

The premiere was polarizing. Some critics called it her most chaotic work. Others—her most human.

"I didn't know what it would become," Lena said. "And I've never felt more honest as an artist."

She had created something from deep care. And then let it go.

Lena's story illustrates a profound creative shift—from controlling outcomes to surrendering to the process. Her earlier works, while technically impressive, were constrained by her need for predictable reception. But when faced with expressing something that truly mattered to her—her sister's experience—she discovered that control was inadequate to the task.

The breakthrough came not from greater control but from its release. By inviting in improvisation, by allowing the dancers to co-create, by opening to uncertainty, she accessed a deeper authenticity. The work became not a showcase for her technical mastery but a genuine expression of something true.

And while the reception was mixed, the satisfaction was complete. Not because everyone applauded, but because she had created from integrity rather than calculation. She had offered something honest rather than manufacturing something safe.

This is the essence of creating without clinging: not abandoning care or craft, but releasing the grip of ego and expectation. Not lowering standards, but changing the relationship with the creative process itself—from domination to collaboration, from certainty to discovery.

The most powerful creative moments often come not when we assert greater control, but when we find the courage to let go.

The Woodworker's Way

Marcus has been making furniture for forty years. His workshop smells of sawdust and linseed oil, with shavings curling on the floor beneath his feet. His hands bear the marks of a lifelong relationship with wood—callused, steady, creased with the grain of time.

When I asked him about his approach to creating, he didn't speak of techniques or designs. He pulled a small wooden box from a shelf and placed it in my hands.

"Feel that," he said.

The box was simple—maple with walnut inlay. But as I held it, I noticed how perfectly it sat in the palm, how the lid opened with a gentle resistance that felt deliberate, how the grain aligned precisely at each corner.

"This one never sold," Marcus explained. "Not fancy enough for the galleries. But it's one of my favorite pieces."

I asked why.

Creating Without Clinging

"Because it's honest," he said. "When I made it, I wasn't thinking about who would buy it or how much I could charge. I was just listening to what the wood wanted to be. See this grain pattern? That told me where to cut. Feel how the edges are slightly rounded? That came from noticing how my own hand wanted to hold it."

Marcus described a creative process guided not by market trends or anticipated reception, but by a conversation with the material itself. His fingers traced the smooth surface as he spoke, touching the wood as one might touch an old friend.

"You can't force wood to be something it's not meant to be. You can only reveal what's already there, waiting."

For Marcus, the joy comes not from praise or sales (though he appreciates both), but from the making itself—from the tactile communion between hand, tool, and material. From the quiet moments when his breathing synchronizes with the rhythm of the plane against grain. From the surprise of discovering a pattern hidden within the timber that no one, not even he, could have predicted.

"Once it leaves my shop, the piece has its own life," he said. "People will see what they see in it. Use it, ignore it, treasure it, discard it. That's not up to me. My job is just to make it as true as I can."

Marcus's approach embodies creating without clinging—a profound care for the work itself combined with a gentle release of its reception. And what emerges from this way of working isn't just beautiful furniture, but a life of sustained creative joy.

Why Outcome Obsession Kills Joy

There's a sneaky shift that happens when we begin to ask, "Will this be successful?" before we even begin.

The Joy of Discontent

The creative self recoils.

Joy turns to pressure.

Flow turns to performance.

And when we create from performance, we're not *in* the act anymore. We're watching ourselves from the outside. We become spectators of our own becoming.

This self-consciousness is the enemy of creative joy. It splits our attention between the work itself and how the work might be perceived. It introduces an inner critic who evaluates every move before it's even complete. It transforms play into production.

Research in psychology reveals that this shift from intrinsic motivation (creating for the joy of creating) to extrinsic motivation (creating for external reward or approval) fundamentally changes the creative experience—and often the quality of what's created.

In a classic study, researchers Teresa Amabile and Beth Hennessey found that when children were told they would be rewarded for drawing pictures, the quality of their artwork declined compared to children who drew purely for enjoyment. The introduction of external incentives actually impaired creativity.

Similar patterns appear in adults. When we create primarily for external validation—for praise, status, or material reward—we tend to take fewer creative risks. We become more conventional, less innovative, less distinctive in our approach. We stick to what we think will work rather than exploring what genuinely interests us.

Even more significantly, this outcome obsession robs us of the intrinsic joy of creation. Instead of being present to the process—to the fascinating problems, the unexpected discoveries, the moments of

Creating Without Clinging

flow—we're constantly measuring, evaluating, projecting into an imagined future where the work is being judged.

I once worked with a novelist who had early success with her first book. Her second book became a torturous process—not because she lacked ideas or skill, but because she couldn't stop imagining how critics would receive each sentence, how readers would compare it to her debut, how her publisher would evaluate its commercial potential.

"I used to lose myself in writing," she told me. "Now I can't stop watching myself write."

Her creative joy had been hijacked by outcome obsession.

We worked together to shift her focus back to the story itself—to the characters she cared about, the questions that intrigued her, the craft challenges that engaged her. Gradually, she rediscovered the immersive joy that had drawn her to writing in the first place.

And paradoxically, when she released her grip on the outcome, her writing became more authentic, more distinctive, more alive.

This pattern repeats across creative domains. The musician who becomes more concerned with streaming numbers than with the music itself. The entrepreneur who focuses more on exit strategy than on creating genuine value. The speaker who cares more about applause than about saying something true.

In each case, outcome obsession doesn't just diminish joy—it often undermines the very outcomes being pursued.

The most resonant creative work typically comes from deep engagement with the process itself, not from calculating what will succeed. The most innovative businesses emerge from genuine passion for solving a problem, not just from chasing market share.

The Joy of Discontent

The most moving speeches spring from authentic conviction, not from techniques designed to manipulate audience response.

Letting go of outcome obsession brings us back inside the moment. Back to *making*.

This doesn't mean we never think about how our work will be received. It doesn't mean we ignore practical realities of audience, market, or context. It means we keep these considerations in their proper place—as factors to be aware of, but not as the primary driving force of our creative process.

The primary driving force remains our own authentic engagement with the work itself—our curiosity, our care, our desire to bring something meaningful into being.

When we create from that place, joy returns. Not because we're guaranteed success, but because we're fully present to the creative act itself. We're in it, not just watching it or managing it.

And that presence is itself a form of joy—one that's available regardless of how the work is ultimately received.

A Practice: The Private Project

Try this:

Start a small creative project with no plan to share it.

- A poem you write just for yourself.
- A song no one will hear.
- A photo series that never leaves your phone.
- A meal you make just for the joy of feeding someone you love.

Notice what shifts.

Notice how the pressure lifts, and presence takes its place.

This is the essence of creating without clinging.

When we remove the possibility of external validation, we're left with the pure relationship between ourselves and the creative act. We discover what we're really doing it for. We learn whether the process itself—regardless of outcome or audience—holds inherent value and joy for us.

Sometimes this experiment reveals surprising insights. We might discover we're more dependent on external validation than we realized. We might notice how habit or expectation, rather than genuine interest, has been driving certain creative choices.

But we might also rediscover a purer form of creative joy—the simple pleasure of making something, of watching it take shape under our hands, of being in conversation with materials or ideas or possibilities.

This private creation becomes a refuge—a space where we can experiment without risk, play without pressure, explore without agenda. It's a laboratory for authentic creative impulse.

And the insights from this private space often transfer to our public creative work. We bring back a remembering of what it feels like to create from intrinsic motivation rather than external pressure. We recover a more grounded relationship with our creative process.

For some, this private creation becomes an ongoing practice—a regular reminder of why we create in the first place. For others, it serves as a reset when outcome obsession has taken over. Either way, it offers a direct experience of creating without clinging.

The ceramicist Paulus Berensohn captured this beautifully when he said, "When you make things you are making meaning, and when we make meaning, we make soul."

The meaning-making, the soul-making—these happen in the process itself. They don't depend on how the finished product is received. They emerge from our willingness to engage fully in the creative act, whether anyone ever sees the results or not.

This doesn't mean all creativity should remain private. It means we benefit from having at least some creative space that's protected from the pressure of public reception—some realm where we create purely for the sake of creating.

From that foundation, we can then bring work into the world not because we need its validation, but because we believe the work itself has something to offer. We can create publicly without clinging because we've remembered the intrinsic value of the creative act.

The Teacher's Offering

Anna has taught high school English for thirty-two years in a quiet Midwestern town. In her classroom, desks are arranged in a circle rather than rows. Sunlight filters through plants on the windowsill. Books line the walls—not just curriculum requirements, but poetry collections, graphic novels, memoirs from diverse voices.

"I used to measure my success by test scores and college acceptances," she told me. "I'd feel crushed when students didn't perform well or when they didn't seem to appreciate what I thought was valuable."

But something shifted twenty years into her teaching career. A former student, James, returned to visit. He'd been in her class a decade earlier—a quiet boy who rarely participated, whose essays were unremarkable. Anna had always considered him one of her "misses"— a student she hadn't managed to reach.

James handed her a dog-eared copy of a novel they'd read in class. "This changed everything for me," he said. "Not right away. It took years. But something you said about this character stuck with me. You said he was brave enough to question his own assumptions, and that's what real courage looks like."

Anna didn't even remember the discussion. It had been a fleeting moment in one class among thousands. But for James, it had been transformative—a seed planted that eventually grew into a way of approaching his life, his work, his relationships.

"That's when I realized I had no idea which moments mattered," Anna said. "The carefully designed lesson that I thought would change lives? Maybe it did nothing. The throwaway comment that I barely considered? Maybe it planted a forest."

This realization transformed her relationship with teaching. She still prepares meticulously, still cares deeply about what happens in her classroom. But she has released her grip on specific outcomes, on knowing exactly what impact she's having or when it might unfold.

"Now I think of teaching as planting a garden where you don't get to see what grows," she smiled. "I'll never know which seeds take root, which ideas bloom years later in conversations I'll never hear. And that's okay. My job is just to plant with care."

Anna's approach doesn't make her less committed—it makes her more present. Free from the constant evaluation of immediate results, she can focus entirely on the quality of what she's offering in each moment. Her creativity in the classroom has flourished precisely because she's stopped measuring its impact.

The Joy of Discontent

"Some of my colleagues burn out because they need constant proof that what they're doing matters," Anna reflected. "But what if the most important things we do are the ones whose effects we never see? What if our greatest contributions are invisible to us?"

Anna's teaching reveals another dimension of creating without clinging—the willingness to offer without witnessing the result. Her classroom is a daily exercise in crafting meaningful experiences and then releasing them completely.

This is not indifference. It's a profound form of care that transcends the need for confirmation. It's the act of creating and offering from a place of abundance rather than need—of giving without demanding to see the return.

And in that release, she has found a sustainable joy that has carried her through decades of teaching, keeping her as passionate and engaged in her final years of teaching as she was in her first.

When We Let Go, We Make Room

Clinging to outcomes tightens the grip. It narrows the field.

But letting go? It opens us up.

It makes space for:

- Surprise.
- Play.
- Imperfection.
- Discovery.

And most of all—it makes room for *joy*.

Not the joy of applause, but the joy of connection—to yourself, to the moment, to the mystery of the creative spark. When we create without clinging, we open ourselves to what wants to emerge rather than forcing what we think should happen. We become partners in the creative process rather than controllers of it. We make room for the unexpected—for the insights, directions, and possibilities we couldn't have planned in advance.

Think of it as a conversation rather than a monologue. When we truly listen—to the materials, to the process, to the work itself—we uncover things we couldn't have known at the outset. As Henry Miller wrote: "The moment one gives close attention to anything, even a blade of grass, it becomes a mysterious, awesome, indescribably magnificent world in itself."

In this listening, we find more interesting, more authentic, more alive creative work than anything we could have predetermined. It allows the work to become what it needs to become, not just what we initially imagined. Martin Scorsese echoes this in film: "There are times when a scene that you thought was absolutely necessary turns out not to be. But what happens in the shooting of the movie is more important than what was conceived of at first."

Even in highly structured creative fields, this letting-go creates space for discovery. Architects design blueprints with precise measurements, but the best understand that the building process itself will reveal needs and opportunities they couldn't have anticipated. They hold the plan firmly enough to guide construction but loosely enough to respond to what emerges.

This balance—between intention and openness, between direction and receptivity—characterizes all creating without clinging. We have purpose, vision, skill. But we also have willingness to be surprised, to follow unexpected threads, to let the work teach us what it wants to be.

And paradoxically, this openness often leads to more meaningful connection with others. When we create authentically, following the work's internal logic rather than calculating audience reaction, we often produce something with unique vitality—something that stands out precisely because it wasn't designed primarily for approval.

As writer Elizabeth Gilbert notes, "The work wants to be made, and it wants to be made through you." When we get our ego and our outcome obsession out of the way, we make room for something beyond ourselves to flow through the creative process.

This doesn't mean ignoring craft or abandoning standards. It means bringing our highest skill to the service of the work itself, rather than using skill merely to achieve predetermined outcomes or external validation.

Creating without clinging is ultimately about trust—trust in the process, trust in what emerges, trust that something valuable can come through us when we get our controlling ego out of the way.

It's also about presence. When we're not fixated on outcomes, we can be fully here—engaged with the creative moment in all its richness, challenge, and possibility.

And that presence itself is joy—a joy not contingent on future recognition or reward, but available right now, in the act of creation itself.

The World Doesn't Need Perfect. It Needs Real.

So many creators get stuck because they're trying to get it right.

But the world isn't waiting for perfect.

It's waiting for *real*. For raw. For honest.

It's waiting for you to show up and make something that matters—to you.

And to trust that if it's meant to ripple outward, it will.

Perfectionism is often disguised clinging—an attempt to control not just the work itself but how it will be received. If I can just make this flawless, the thinking goes, then it will be immune to criticism. Then it will be worthy. Then I will be worthy.

But this pursuit of perfection often leads to creative paralysis. We never start because the gap between what we imagine and what we can currently execute feels too large. Or we never finish because the work never measures up to our impossible standard.

Even worse, perfectionism can lead to work that's technically impressive but emotionally sterile. In polishing away every flaw, we often remove the very humanity that allows others to connect with what we've made.

What moves people isn't technical perfection. It's authenticity. Vulnerability. The sense that a real human being, with all their complexity and contradiction, made this thing as an expression of what matters to them.

Think of your favorite book, song, film, or artwork. Chances are, what you respond to isn't its flawlessness but its truth—the way it captures something essential about human experience, the way it makes you feel seen or understood or less alone.

Leonard Cohen expressed this perfectly in his song "Anthem": "Ring the bells that still can ring / Forget your perfect offering / There is a crack in everything / That's how the light gets in."

The cracks—the imperfections, the places where our humanity shows through—are often precisely what allow others to connect with our creative work.

This doesn't mean we abandon standards or stop developing our craft. It means we recognize that technical skill serves the deeper purpose of authentic expression, not the other way around.

The paradox is that when we stop trying to be perfect—when we create to express rather than to impress—we often produce work that resonates more deeply with others. We communicate not just ideas or images or sounds, but the lived human experience behind them. We create not perfect artifacts, but authentic connections.

I've seen this play out countless times with the creators I work with. The writer who finally stops trying to sound impressive and simply writes the story they can't stop thinking about. The musician who stops chasing trends and creates the album they genuinely want to hear. The designer who breaks from convention to make something that personally excites them.

In each case, releasing the need for perfection—for universal approval, for objective "rightness"—freed them to create something far more compelling than their pursuit of flawlessness ever could have produced.

Create.

Release.

Begin again.

This rhythm—of showing up authentically, offering what you have, and then letting go—is the heart of creating without clinging. It's not a one-time achievement but an ongoing practice, a relationship with the creative process that generates not just meaningful work, but a meaningful life.

The world doesn't need your perfect offering. It needs your truth, your unique perspective, your willingness to make something real rather than wait until it's flawless.

And you don't need perfection, either. You need the joy that comes from authentic creation—from being fully engaged in bringing something meaningful into being, regardless of how it's ultimately received.

The joy is in the creating.

The meaning is in the making.

The beauty is in showing up, again and again, with open hands and an open heart.

Not clinging.

Just creating.

Eastern Wisdom in Action: Non-Attachment in Creative Practice

Creating without clinging isn't just a philosophical concept. It's a practical approach that transforms both the experience of creating and often the quality of what's created.

Consider these concrete practices drawn from Eastern wisdom and adapted for contemporary creative work:

Begin with intention, end with release. Before starting a creative session, take a moment to set an intention focused on the process rather than the outcome. Perhaps: "I intend to stay present to what wants to emerge" or "I intend to create with openness and care." Then, when the session ends, consciously release attachment to what you've made with a simple gesture or phrase. Some creators literally open their hands as a physical reminder of this release.

Practice the "beginner's mind." The Zen concept of shoshin or "beginner's mind" invites us to approach each creative act with fresh eyes, free from preconceptions about how it "should" go or what the outcome "should" be. Even if you've been working in your field for decades, can you bring a sense of discovery to today's work? Can you be willing to not know exactly where it's going?

Separate creation from evaluation. Many creative processes benefit from clearly separating the generative phase (creating) from the evaluative phase (assessing and refining). When these blur together, clinging often follows. Try timeboxing: "For the next 30 minutes, I'll just create without judging. Later, I can review with discernment."

Embrace impermanence. Some creative practices intentionally incorporate impermanence to practice non-attachment. Sand mandalas in Tibetan Buddhism are created with elaborate care over days, then ceremonially destroyed to symbolize impermanence. You might create something beautiful knowing it's temporary, or practice letting go of work you've become too attached to.

Use constraints as liberation. Paradoxically, constraints often increase creative freedom by removing the paralysis of too many options. Setting parameters for your work—time limits, material restrictions, formal requirements—can reduce self-consciousness and outcome fixation, allowing more spontaneous engagement.

Practice gratitude for the process. At the end of a creative session, regardless of how you feel about what you've made, take a moment to appreciate the opportunity to create at all. This shifts focus from outcome evaluation to gratitude for the process itself—a powerful antidote to clinging.

CREATING WITHOUT CLINGING

These practices don't eliminate care or commitment. They transform how we relate to our work—from grasping to holding, from demanding to offering, from controlling to collaborating.

As the Tao Te Ching suggests: "Do your work, then step back. The only path to serenity."

Reflection: Where Are You Clinging?

Take a moment to reflect on your own creative process:

- Where do you notice yourself clinging to specific outcomes?
- How does this clinging affect your creative experience? Your joy? Your willingness to take risks?
- What would it look like to care deeply about your work without clinging to how it's received?
- What small step could you take today to practice creating without clinging?

Remember: The goal isn't to stop caring. It's to care in a way that liberates rather than constricts—that allows both you and the work to breathe.

Creating without clinging isn't something you achieve once and for all. It's a practice—one you return to again and again as you navigate the creative journey.

But each time you notice yourself clinging and gently open your hands, you create more space for joy, for discovery, for the work to become what it needs to become.

And that openness—that willingness to engage fully without grasping—might be the greatest creative skill of all.

To create freely is a quiet rebellion. But sometimes, joy needs to be louder. Sometimes, the most radical thing we can do is bring beauty,

THE JOY OF DISCONTENT

presence, and care into places that seem to resist them. That's where we're headed next.

CHAPTER 5

Joy as Rebellion

> ***Refusal***
> *I refuse to go quiet*
> *into the gray of should.*
> *I choose color,*
> *motion,*
> *wild belief.*
> *This joy is not escape—*
> *it's revolt.*

There's a kind of joy the world doesn't always understand.

It doesn't look like comfort.

It doesn't sound like politeness.

It doesn't play by the rules of "fit in, stay small, do what you're told."

This kind of joy burns.

It rises out of discontent—not to destroy, but to build.

It looks at the dullness of conformity, the ache of injustice, the dead weight of routine—and says:

No. Not like this. There must be another way.

And then, quietly or loudly, it begins to create that way.

The Radical Act of Caring

In a culture built on distraction, cynicism, and self-preservation, *to care deeply is a rebellious act.*

It's easier to coast.

To disengage.

To numb ourselves with productivity or scrolling or safe, stale rhythms.

But joy—real joy—asks more of us. It asks us to be *awake.* To feel the tension. To notice what's broken and still dare to show up with light.

The joy of discontent is not naïve.

It is forged in the fire of *noticing too much—and refusing to look away.*

Consider what we're up against. We live in what sociologist Hartmut Rosa calls an "acceleration society"—a world moving so rapidly that meaningful connection becomes increasingly difficult. Technology bombards us with stimuli designed to capture attention without deepening engagement. Economic systems reward extraction over regeneration, efficiency over presence, growth over meaning.

Against this backdrop, disengagement becomes a natural defense. Why care too deeply about anything when everything is moving too fast to hold? Why invest emotionally in what seems beyond our power to change? Why feel the full weight of the world's complexity when numbness offers such convenient relief?

These questions aren't abstract. They're lived daily in our decisions to look away from suffering, to accept destructive systems as inevitable, to retreat into private comfort when public engagement feels too demanding.

The poet and activist Audre Lorde recognized this pattern decades ago: "The master's tools will never dismantle the master's house." One of those tools is emotional disengagement—the learned capacity to stop caring as a way of surviving within systems that don't value care.

But what if caring itself—deep, stubborn, inconvenient caring—is the most rebellious act available to us?

To care in a world that rewards detachment is to declare that something matters more than convenience, more than comfort, more than fitting in. It's to plant a flag in the ground of your own values and say: This matters enough to feel uncomfortable about. This matters enough to stay awake for.

This quality of care doesn't always announce itself loudly. It can be quiet, persistent, even gentle. But make no mistake—it is radical.

The teacher who refuses to treat students as test scores, who sees their humanity even within dehumanizing systems. The designer who insists on sustainability when planned obsolescence would be more profitable. The parent who creates technology-free zones of genuine connection in a household bombarded by digital distraction.

Each is engaged in rebellion—not through protest (though that has its place), but through the simple, powerful act of caring when it would be easier not to.

Joanna Macy, the environmental activist and Buddhist scholar, calls this "active hope"—not the hope that everything will work out, but the choice to act as if our actions matter even without guarantees. She describes: Active hope is a practice... it involves three steps: First, we take a clear view of reality; second, we identify what we hope for; and third, we take steps to move in that direction.

This sequence—seeing clearly, hoping actively, moving deliberately—is precisely the pathway from discontent to joy. Not the shallow joy of denial or distraction, but the deeper joy that comes from aligning action with values, regardless of outcome.

The Croatian theologian Miroslav Volf speaks of practicing joy 'against the evidence'—not because things are perfect, but because joy itself becomes a form of resistance against forces that would prefer we remain numb, compliant, and disengaged.

To care deeply is to refuse that numbness. To feel joy in that caring—even when it hurts, even when it disrupts—is perhaps the most rebellious choice we can make.

The joy of discontent is not about putting on a happy face despite everything. It's about allowing yourself to feel what matters so much that you're moved to create something in response. It's about refusing the gray deadness of disengagement and choosing instead the vibrant aliveness of care.

This is not comfortable joy. It's not safe joy. But it might be the most human joy available to us—the joy of being fully awake in a world that often prefers we stay asleep.

Discontent as the Spark of Change

History is filled with makers, leaders, and everyday people whose joy was a response to what they couldn't accept.

- The architect who rebuilt beauty after war.
- The teacher who reimagined education in the face of inequality.

- The founder who started a company not to "disrupt," but to *heal.*

Their joy wasn't blind optimism.

It was forged in discomfort—and it became creative resistance.

They didn't settle for a broken world.

They didn't become bitter.

They made something better.

This pattern—of discontent sparking creative action that ultimately generates joy—repeats throughout human history, across cultures and contexts.

Consider the Impressionist painters of 19th century France. Rejected by the official Salon with its rigid academic standards, these artists didn't give up or conform. They created their own exhibitions. They developed new techniques that captured light, motion, and everyday experience in ways the establishment couldn't recognize as valuable. Their discontent with the status quo wasn't just complaint—it was the catalyst for a revolutionary approach to seeing and depicting the world.

Consider Wangari Maathai, who founded the Green Belt Movement in Kenya. Facing environmental degradation, women's disempowerment, and political corruption, she didn't surrender to despair. She organized women to plant trees—more than 51 million of them. Her discontent sparked action, her action built community, and that community transformed not just the landscape but the social fabric.

These examples aren't about heroic individuals with superhuman abilities. They're about ordinary people who refused to accept what others told them was inevitable. Their discontent wasn't a personality

The Joy of Discontent

flaw or a failure to adjust—it was a creative spark that ignited meaningful change.

But there's an important distinction here. Not all discontent leads to creative action. Some hardens into bitterness, calcifies into cynicism, or dissolves into apathy. What makes the difference?

Research in psychology offers some clues. Studies on "constructive discontent" versus "destructive discontent" suggest that the critical factor is how we relate to our dissatisfaction.

Constructive discontent maintains connection—to others, to meaning, to possibility. It sees beyond what is broken to what could be created. It channels frustration into imagination and action rather than rumination or blame.

Destructive discontent, by contrast, breaks connection. It isolates, withdraws, attacks without creating alternatives. It focuses exclusively on what's wrong without envisioning what could be right.

The difference isn't in how strongly we feel dissatisfaction. The difference is in what we do with it.

The anthropologist Margaret Mead's famous quote speaks to this: "Never doubt that a small group of thoughtful, committed citizens can change the world; indeed, it's the only thing that ever has." What makes these citizens effective isn't just their commitment, it's their thoughtfulness, their capacity to transform discontent into creative action.

This transformative capacity isn't reserved for world-historical movements or grand artistic innovations. It operates in everyday life, in small but significant ways.

The parent dissatisfied with available children's books who starts writing their own stories at the kitchen table. The community member frustrated by food waste who organizes a neighborhood composting system. The office worker tired of sterile environments who brings plants and creates gathering spaces that nurture connection.

Each begins with discontent—with the tension between what is and what could be. But instead of turning away or giving up, they turn toward that tension and create something in response.

This is how joy emerges from discontent. Not by bypassing the difficult feelings, but by honoring them enough to respond creatively. Not by settling for what is, but by engaging fully with what could be.

As writer and activist Rebecca Solnit observes, in essence: Joy doesn't betray but sustains activism. And when you face a politics that aspires to make you fearful, alienated and isolated, joy is a fine initial act of insurrection.

That insurrection begins with the courage to feel discontent fully— not as a burden to escape, but as a spark to kindle.

The Neighborhood Garden:
A Collective Response

In the shadow of three towering apartment buildings, a vacant lot had collected debris for decades. Broken glass, fast-food wrappers, and discarded furniture formed a monument to urban neglect. Residents hurried past, eyes averted, as if the ugliness might be contagious.

Maria had lived in the middle building for fifteen years, her kitchen window overlooking the wasteland. "Every morning, I'd look out and feel this weight," she told me. "Not just sadness, but a kind of anger. Why should we have to live with this? Why should our children think this is normal?"

The Joy of Discontent

The discontent was collective—felt by dozens of residents but rarely discussed. It was the kind of shared resignation that settles into neglected communities, the tacit acceptance that some places simply don't deserve beauty.

But during a particularly harsh winter, something shifted. Maria invited neighbors for coffee and asked a simple question: "What if we did something about that lot ourselves?"

The first meeting drew eight people. The second, fifteen. By the third, they had a plan forming. Not a formal proposal to authorities, but a direct response: they would transform the space themselves.

They began small—clearing trash on Saturdays, bringing tools from home. They faced skepticism ("It'll just get trashed again"), bureaucratic hurdles (navigating city permissions), and their own doubts about what was possible.

But they kept showing up. A retired contractor taught younger residents how to build raised beds. A nurse organized a seedling exchange. Children designed painted signs and rock borders. What began as a cleanup evolved into a true community garden—with vegetables, flowers, benches, and eventually a small playground.

"The joy wasn't in completing it," Maria explained. "It was in seeing someone's grandmother teaching teenagers how to plant tomatoes. It was in neighbors who had lived next door for years finally learning each other's names. It was in my son saying he wants to be a landscape architect."

The garden became more than a beautification project. It became a physical manifestation of collective refusal—a declaration that this community deserved beauty, deserved connection, deserved care. Their shared discontent became a creative force, transforming not just the landscape but the community's relationship with itself.

"We didn't wait for permission to care about where we live," said Carlos, a longtime resident who discovered a passion for composting through the project. "That's what makes it revolutionary. We decided our neighborhood deserved better, so we made it better. Together."

The garden still requires maintenance. Conflicts still arise over design decisions and responsibilities. But something fundamental has changed in how residents relate to their shared space and to each other. Their collective joy wasn't about reaching a perfect endpoint but about actively creating something that embodies their values—about transforming resignation into creative power.

This is collective joy as rebellion—not a fleeting emotion, but an ongoing practice of creating alternatives to what exists, of insisting on beauty and connection in places designed for neither.

Story: The Quiet Architect

There's a woman I know—an urban designer—who began her career building luxury condos. The money was good. The praise was steady. But the work left her hollow.

Then she took a year off. She walked her city. Listened. Sat in public housing complexes. Talked to teenagers, single moms, retirees. She noticed what the city forgot.

Now she designs inclusive, dignified public spaces—not for prestige, but because she *refuses* to let joy be a luxury good.

Her discontent became her blueprint. Her joy is in the making.

Elena didn't plan to become what she calls "an architect of the forgotten spaces." Her career had followed a predictable upward trajectory—prestigious university, competitive internships, eventual partnership in a firm known for sleek, expensive developments that transformed urban skylines.

The Joy of Discontent

"I was doing everything right," she told me. "My parents were proud. My bank account was growing. My work was winning awards."

But something felt increasingly wrong. The disconnect crystallized one evening when she attended a gala celebrating the opening of her firm's latest project—a gleaming residential tower with multi-million dollar units. From the rooftop bar, she could see directly into the windows of a public housing complex just ten blocks away, where residents had no access to green space, where playgrounds had been abandoned to disrepair, where shared spaces fostered isolation rather than connection.

"I realized I was using my training to create beautiful spaces for people who already had access to beauty," she said. "Meanwhile, the majority of the city was treated as if their need for beauty, for dignity in their surroundings, was somehow less important."

The discontent grew until she couldn't ignore it. Against the advice of mentors and the concern of family, she took what she called a "sabbatical of listening." For months, she simply explored areas of the city she'd never really seen, despite having lived there for a decade. She sat in parks and plazas, observing how different spaces fostered or hindered human connection. She interviewed residents about what they loved and what they longed for in their neighborhoods.

What she discovered wasn't surprising, exactly, but it was transformative. People universally desired spaces that reflected their dignity, that facilitated connection, that offered both refuge and possibility. This wasn't a luxury—it was a fundamental human need, as essential as shelter itself.

"I realized that joy in public space isn't frivolous—it's necessary," Elena explained. "And the fact that it's systematically denied to certain communities isn't just an oversight. It's a form of violence."

Rather than returning to her old firm with new ideas, Elena founded her own practice with a radical approach. She would work primarily in underserved communities, designing public spaces with the same attention to beauty, functionality, and human experience that typically went into luxury developments. She would prioritize projects that community members themselves identified as meaningful. And she would measure success not by awards or profit, but by how spaces were actually used and valued by the people who lived with them.

It hasn't been easy. Funding is always a challenge. Bureaucratic resistance is constant. The work is often slow and unglamorous.

But the joy is palpable. Not the fleeting satisfaction of external validation, but the deeper joy of aligning work with values. The joy of watching children discover a playground designed for their actual needs. The joy of seeing elders gather in a plaza that honors their presence. The joy of creating beauty that belongs to everyone.

"I'm not naive," Elena says. "I know a well-designed public space doesn't solve structural inequality or eliminate racism or fix the housing crisis. But it does something real. It says to a community: You deserve beauty. You deserve dignity. You deserve spaces made with care."

Her discontent didn't lead to disengagement. It led to reconceiving what architecture could be and whom it could serve. It led to joy—not despite the challenges, but because of her creative response to them.

This is the pattern of joyful rebellion. Not denying what's broken, but refusing to accept it as inevitable. Not escaping discomfort, but allowing it to spark creative engagement. Not settling for how things are, but imagining and then building how they could be.

The joy isn't in pretending everything is fine. The joy is in the making of something better.

Choosing Joy When It's Easier Not To

Some days, it's easier to disengage. To shrug off the ache. To believe our effort doesn't matter.

But creating, leading, building from a place of joy—in a world that often rewards disconnection—is a radical thing.

It says:

- I see the cracks, and I still care.
- I feel the weight, and I still choose wonder.
- I'm not waiting for permission to be fully alive.

This is not surface joy. This is depth joy. Root joy.

There's a persistent misconception about joy: that it's essentially passive, something that happens to us under favorable circumstances. That it arrives when conditions are right and departs when they're challenging. That it's a reward for ease rather than a resource for difficulty.

But what if joy is actually a choice? Not in a simplistic "just be happy" sense that denies legitimate suffering, but in a deeper sense—a commitment to remain engaged with life's beauty and possibility even in the midst of its brokenness.

This kind of chosen joy isn't about putting on a mask of positivity. It's about a fundamental orientation toward life that refuses to let difficulty have the final word. It's about insisting on creating meaning even when meaning isn't handed to us.

Joy as Rebellion

The Austrian psychiatrist and Holocaust survivor Viktor Frankl wrote profoundly about this in "Man's Search for Meaning." Even in the concentration camps, he observed that some prisoners found ways to maintain their inner freedom—to choose their response to unimaginable suffering. "Everything can be taken from a man but one thing," he wrote, "the last of the human freedoms—to choose one's attitude in any given set of circumstances, to choose one's own way."

This isn't to minimize suffering or suggest that joy is always equally accessible regardless of circumstances. Systemic oppression, trauma, poverty, and illness create very real barriers to joy. But within whatever space remains for choice—and that space varies widely depending on privilege and circumstance—the decision to orient toward joy rather than resignation becomes a powerful act of human dignity.

The civil rights leader Howard Thurman spoke of this: "Don't ask what the world needs. Ask what makes you come alive and go do it. Because what the world needs is people who have come alive."

Coming alive—choosing engagement over numbness, creativity over resignation, wonder over cynicism—is at the heart of joyful rebellion. It's not a single decision but a practice, one we return to again and again as circumstances challenge our capacity for joy.

This practice becomes especially important in times of collective crisis or chronic stress. When the news cycle is relentlessly grim, when systems seem too entrenched to change, when personal challenges accumulate without resolution—these are precisely the moments when choosing joy becomes both most difficult and most necessary.

Research in positive psychology suggests that this kind of chosen joy isn't just psychologically beneficial—it's practically effective. Studies by Barbara Fredrickson and others show that positive emotions broaden our perceptual field and build cognitive resources. We literally see more options, think more flexibly, and access more creative solutions when we maintain connection to positive emotional states, including joy.

This doesn't mean ignoring problems or pretending everything is fine. It means approaching challenges from a place of engaged aliveness rather than defeated resignation. It means refusing to let difficulty shrink our capacity for wonder, connection, and meaning.

The poet Jack Gilbert captures this beautifully in his poem "A Brief for the Defense":

"We must risk delight. We can do without pleasure,

but not delight. Not enjoyment. We must have

the stubbornness to accept our gladness in the ruthless

furnace of this world."

This stubborn gladness isn't naïveté. It's a clear-eyed insistence on remaining fully human in a world that often incentivizes partial humanity—the parts that produce, consume, and conform, but not the parts that dream, create, and connect.

Choosing joy in this context isn't easy. It requires swimming against powerful currents of cynicism, detachment, and resignation. It means being willing to look foolish or naive in a culture that often equates sophistication with detached irony.

But this choice—to care deeply, to engage fully, to insist on wonder even in difficult circumstances—is precisely what keeps us human in dehumanizing systems. It's what allows us to imagine and then create alternatives to what exists.

This is why joy is rebellion. Not because it denies reality, but because it refuses to let reality have the last word. Because it insists there is always something we can create, something we can offer, some way we can enlarge life rather than shrink from it.

As philosopher Cornel West puts it: "Joy is different from happiness. Happiness is tied to our circumstances, whether things are going up or down. Joy is a steadfastness... the courage to rejoice when times are tough."

This courage doesn't come easily. But it comes. Through practice. Through community. Through the daily choice to remain engaged rather than withdraw, to create rather than merely critique, to insist on beauty even in the broken places.

That choice—made and remade each day—is at the heart of joyful rebellion.

REBELLION THROUGH BEAUTY

Art has always known this truth: beauty can be a form of protest.

To write a poem in a war zone.

To paint on a crumbling wall.

To dance where dancing is forbidden.

To speak love into structures that thrive on fear.

These are not soft gestures.

They are declarations: *We are still human. We still feel. We still imagine.*

The creative act becomes the resistance.

And joy becomes the flag we fly.

The Joy of Discontent

Throughout history, beauty has served not just as decoration but as declaration—a way of insisting on dignity, possibility, and alternative visions in the face of dehumanizing forces.

The murals that transform concrete barriers into stories of liberation. The gardens planted in abandoned lots. The music that gives voice to truths official narratives try to silence. The community rituals that preserve cultural memory against forces of erasure.

In each case, beauty serves not as escape from harsh realities but as response to them—a refusal to accept ugliness, degradation, or forgetting as inevitable.

The Polish poet Zbigniew Herbert wrote, in essence, during the oppressive Communist regime: You have to create your own aesthetic, against the void, against the horror, even when it isn't much use. You have to leave a trace—because we are all writing on sand with a stick that will break.

This act—of leaving a beauty trace against the void—has sustained human dignity through history's darkest chapters. During the Holocaust, prisoners in concentration camps created art from scraps, composed music, recited poetry from memory. Not because these acts would save them from physical death, but because they preserved something essential about what it means to be human.

The Argentine Mothers of the Plaza de Mayo marched silently in circles, wearing white headscarves embroidered with the names of their 'disappeared' children during the military dictatorship. Their choice of aesthetic—circular formation, white scarves against dark circumstances—transformed their grief into a powerful visual testament that eventually helped bring down a regime.

JOY AS REBELLION

In South Africa during apartheid, music and dance became vehicles not just for expressing opposition but for imagining and embodying the more just society activists were fighting to create. As Archbishop Desmond Tutu often observed, protest songs weren't just about anger—they contained joy, even amid suffering, because they connected people to a vision larger than the present reality.

These examples aren't exceptions. They represent a consistent human response to oppression, violence, and dehumanization: the creation of beauty not as decoration, but as declaration of what remains inviolable in the human spirit.

This isn't about aestheticizing suffering or suggesting that art alone can solve structural problems. It's about recognizing that beauty—intentionally created and shared—serves essential functions in human resistance and resilience.

Beauty reminds us of what's possible beyond current constraints. It preserves cultural memory when official narratives attempt erasure. It creates moments of connection in contexts designed for isolation. It insists on dignity when systems attempt degradation.

And perhaps most importantly, beauty creates joy—not the shallow happiness of forgetting what's broken, but the deeper joy of remaining fully alive to both suffering and possibility. The joy that comes from refusing to let circumstances determine the full measure of your humanity.

The writer and activist adrienne maree brown speaks of 'pleasure activism'—the deliberate cultivation of joy, connection, and delight as essential aspects of working for justice. She writes, in essence, that pleasure and joy—particularly the pleasure and joy of being in harmony with each other and the planet—are part of the world we are

The Joy of Discontent

trying to create. "Part of our work is to make justice and liberation irresistible," she adds.

This making of justice and liberation "irresistible" isn't about denying their difficulty. It's about insisting that the world we're working toward isn't just about the absence of oppression but the presence of beauty, connection, and joy.

The rebellion lies in refusing to postpone joy until after some future victory. It lies in claiming joy now, as part of the creative resistance itself.

This is what sets joyful rebellion apart from mere opposition. Opposition defines itself primarily against what it rejects. Joyful rebellion certainly includes critique—but it moves beyond critique to creation. It articulates alternatives. It embodies, however imperfectly, the values it seeks in the wider world.

In this way, joy itself becomes both means and end—both the path and the destination. We don't fight for a world of justice and beauty so that someday, finally, we might experience joy. We bring joy into the fight itself, as a form of prefigurative politics—embodying in our present resistance the qualities we seek in the future we're working toward.

This is the invitation of joyful rebellion: not to wait for perfect conditions, but to create beauty now, where you are, with what you have. Not because it solves everything, but because it matters. Because it declares that no matter what forces attempt to diminish human dignity, something in us remains sovereign, creative, and free.

The creative act becomes the resistance.

And joy becomes the flag we fly.

A Practice: Ask What You Refuse to Accept

Try this:

Write down one thing you cannot accept about the world—or your world.

Then ask:

- What kind of beauty could I create in response to this?
- What kind of light could I offer, even if it feels small?
- What could I build that becomes a quiet rebellion?

Your joy is not separate from your fire.

It is how your fire *moves through you*.

This practice isn't about generating a perfect answer or immediate solution. It's about training your capacity to move from discontent to creation—from noticing what you cannot accept to imagining what you might offer in response.

The key is specificity. Rather than being overwhelmed by everything that needs changing, focus on one particular aspect of the world (or your world) that you find unacceptable. It might be something global or something local. Something systemic or something personal. What matters is that it genuinely matters to you—that you feel a real emotional response to this unacceptable condition.

Once you've identified this point of discontent, allow yourself to feel it fully. Don't rush to fix or resolve. Simply acknowledge: This matters to me. This feels unacceptable.

Then, shift from problem to possibility. Ask not just "What's wrong?" but "What could be created in response?" This doesn't mean your creation must directly solve the problem. It might offer an alternative vision. It might preserve what's being threatened. It might simply bear witness to what matters.

The beauty you create could take countless forms. It might be artistic—a poem, a painting, a song, a garden. It might be relational—a new way of connecting with others, a community gathering, a different approach to conversation. It might be structural—a program, an organization, a changed policy in your workplace or community.

What matters isn't the scale or the form, but the movement from passive discontent to creative response. From merely observing what's unacceptable to offering something in its place.

This practice builds the core muscle of joyful rebellion: the capacity to transform awareness into creation, to channel the energy of discontent into the energy of making.

And as you practice this movement—from discontent to creation, from observation to offering—you may discover something surprising: joy emerges not in spite of your clear-eyed awareness of what's broken, but because of your creative response to it.

Your joy is not separate from your fire.

It is how your fire *moves through you.*

Joy Doesn't Need Permission

You don't have to wait until things are fixed.

You don't need to earn your right to create, lead, play, build.

You can begin now.

Right in the middle of the mess.

Joy as Rebellion

The world needs people who feel deeply—and still move forward with heart.

Not because it's easy. But because it matters.

There's a persistent myth in our culture: that joy is something we arrive at after problems are solved, after conditions are perfect, after we've checked enough boxes or fixed enough flaws.

This myth shows up in countless ways. The retirement savings commercial that suggests real living begins after decades of work. The beauty industry that implies joy awaits on the other side of perfected appearance. The self-improvement paradigm that positions happiness as the reward for becoming a "better version" of yourself.

These narratives share a common structure: joy exists somewhere else, after something is resolved. It's conditional, contingent, available only under the right circumstances.

But what if this entire premise is backward? What if joy isn't what we get after creating better conditions, but what empowers us to create those conditions in the first place?

This is the radical reframe offered by joyful rebellion: joy doesn't come after. Joy comes through. It's not the reward for fixing what's broken—it's the resource that sustains us while we engage with brokenness.

This doesn't mean we should deny difficulties or pretend everything is fine when it isn't. It means we can claim joy even in the midst of working for change—not as escape from reality, but as fuel for engaging with it more fully.

The writer and activist Audre Lorde spoke powerfully to this when, while battling cancer, she wrote: "Caring for myself is not self-indulgence, it is self-preservation, and that is an act of political warfare." For Lorde, claiming joy and pleasure wasn't separate from her justice work—it was integral to it, a way of refusing the depletion that systems of oppression count on to maintain themselves.

This perspective transforms how we think about creating change—whether in our personal lives, our communities, or our world. We don't have to choose between acknowledging problems and experiencing joy. We can do both simultaneously. In fact, the deepest joy often emerges precisely in the act of engaging creatively with what matters most.

Consider the climate activists who plant community gardens—not just as symbolic gestures, but as concrete examples of the world they're working toward. Or the prison abolitionists who create restorative justice circles that embody alternatives to punitive systems. Or the educators who design learning environments based on curiosity and collaboration rather than competition and standardization.

In each case, they're not waiting for conditions to be perfect before experiencing the joy of the values they champion. They're bringing those values into their current work, finding joy in the creating itself—even as they acknowledge how much remains to be transformed.

This is the essential insight of joyful rebellion: we don't have to wait for permission to experience joy. We don't have to earn it through perfect circumstances or perfect action. We can claim it now, as our birthright—not despite the broken world, but as part of our creative engagement with it.

The musician and activist Toshi Reagon puts it, in essence: I've dedicated my life to doing things that take a very long time. I must find joy in the day-to-day work of it—I can't just be waiting for the result.

This daily claiming of joy isn't frivolous or indulgent. It's necessary. It's what allows us to sustain commitment to change that might take generations. It's what helps us resist the burnout, cynicism, and despair that so often derail efforts toward greater justice and beauty.

The world needs people who feel deeply—who refuse the numbing effects of overwhelm, who maintain their capacity for both sorrow and joy, who engage with the full spectrum of human experience rather than reducing themselves to mere functionaries within broken systems.

And the world needs people who move forward with heart—who respond to what they see not with paralysis or rage alone, but with creative action rooted in love for what's possible.

This combination—deep feeling and heart-centered action—is the essence of joyful rebellion. It's not easy. It requires swimming against powerful currents of cynicism, detachment, and resignation. It means being willing to appear naive or foolish in a culture that often equates sophistication with detached irony.

But this choice—to care deeply, to engage fully, to insist on joy even in difficult circumstances—is precisely what keeps us human in dehumanizing systems. It's what allows us to imagine and then create alternatives to what exists.

You don't have to wait until things are fixed.

You don't need to earn your right to create, lead, play, build.

You can begin now.

Right in the middle of the mess.

THE JOY OF DISCONTENT

Joy, when practiced in the face of discontent, becomes a kind of grace. And grace doesn't always finish what it starts. In the next chapter, we'll explore how to make peace with the unfinished—and why that may be the most human act of all.

The joy is in the becoming.

CHAPTER 6

The Beautiful Unfinished

Becoming
Leave the paint wet.
Let the song trail off.
Walk without knowing the last line.
The masterpiece was never the thing---
it was the motion of your hand,
the ache in your heart,
the breath that said:
still here.

We live in a culture obsessed with finishing.

Projects. Books. Careers. The self.

But there's something sacred in what remains unfinished. Something *human* in the cracks, the drafts, the incomplete thoughts.

Perfection is sterile. Completion is temporary.

THE JOY OF DISCONTENT

But the *unfinished*---it's alive.

To live in the joy of discontent is to stop fearing the undone.

To let your life be a draft, your work a process, your self a canvas still in motion.

THE PIRAHÃ AND THE LANGUAGE OF NOW

There's a tribe in the Amazon---the **Pirahã**---whose language has no fixed past or future tense. Studied by linguist **Daniel Everett**, their culture challenges everything we think we know about time, purpose, and satisfaction.

The Pirahã don't speak of what happened long ago.

They don't make plans for far-off futures.

They live in the *immediacy of experience*.

And they are, by many accounts, among the happiest people on Earth.

They don't measure life by completion.

They live by *presence*.

There's a lesson here. A quiet reminder that joy isn't in arriving---it's in *inhabiting*.

When Daniel Everett first went to live with the Pirahã in the 1970s, he went as a missionary, intent on translating the Bible into their language. What he discovered instead was a worldview so radically different from his own that it ultimately transformed his understanding of language, consciousness, and what it means to be human.

The Pirahã language, Everett found, lacks several features considered universal in human languages---including numbers, fixed color terms, and most strikingly, recursive grammar (the ability to embed clauses within clauses). But perhaps the most profound difference was their relationship to time.

The Pirahã have what linguists call an "immediacy of experience" principle. They generally don't discuss events they haven't witnessed firsthand or that haven't been directly reported by a witness. Their conversations focus overwhelmingly on what's happening now, with limited reference to distant past or future.

This isn't due to cognitive limitation---the Pirahã are capable of understanding temporal concepts when needed. Rather, it reflects a cultural value placed on immediate experience rather than abstract time. Their happiness doesn't depend on remembered achievements or anticipated completions. It emerges from full engagement with the present moment.

What's remarkable about the Pirahã is their contentment despite (or perhaps because of) this orientation. They don't experience the chronic dissatisfaction that often characterizes achievement-oriented cultures---the nagging sense that life would be better after the next accomplishment, the next acquisition, the next milestone.

As Everett writes in Don't Sleep, There Are Snakes, "the Pirahã 'show no evidence of depression, chronic anxiety, or suicide." They do not depend on external validation for their happiness, he observes.

This doesn't mean their lives are free from hardship. They face the significant challenges of living in a demanding environment, including food scarcity, disease, and external threats to their way of life. But their response to these challenges doesn't involve the future-oriented striving that characterizes much of modern existence.

The Pirahã's approach finds fascinating parallels in other cultures. In Japan, the aesthetic tradition of *wabi-sabi* embraces the beauty of the imperfect, impermanent, and incomplete. Rather than seeing incompletion as a flaw, wabi-sabi recognizes it as a fundamental truth of existence. The cracked tea bowl, the asymmetrical arrangement, the weather-worn gate---these aren't failed attempts at perfection but expressions of a deeper beauty that accepts the transient nature of all things.

Wabi-sabi emerged from Zen Buddhist philosophy, which emphasizes that nothing is finished, nothing is perfect, and nothing lasts. Yet rather than responding to this reality with despair, the tradition finds profound beauty and meaning in precisely these qualities. The cherry blossoms are treasured not despite their brief blooming but because of it. The handmade object is valued not despite its irregularities but because of them.

Both the Pirahã's temporal immediacy and Japan's wabi-sabi aesthetics challenge Western culture's fixation on completion and permanence. They suggest alternative paths to joy---not through arriving at some imagined endpoint, but through fully inhabiting the unfolding present.

These perspectives invite us not to abandon our goals or projects, but to hold them differently. To recognize that the joy isn't in the finishing, but in the making. Not in having arrived, but in being fully present to the journey.

There's a lesson here. A quiet reminder that joy isn't in arriving---it's in *inhabiting*.

COMPLETION IS A CONCEPT. CREATION IS A STATE.

We think we want to be done.

But what we actually want is *to be in it*---to be engaged, lit up, moving.

Done is static.

Creation is dynamic.

And creation requires the willingness to keep going, even when the end isn't in sight.

Some of the most meaningful things in life---the relationships, the visions, the callings---never reach a finish line.

They unfold.

They deepen.

They shift shape.

To love something is to let it evolve.

The notion of completion is seductive. It promises relief, achievement, proof of worthiness. It suggests a stopping point---a moment when we can finally rest, knowing we've arrived.

But this concept of "done" is largely artificial. Look closely at anything we consider complete, and you'll find ongoing processes beneath the surface. The "finished" book continues to evolve in the minds of its readers. The "completed" building begins its long conversation with weather, inhabitants, and time. The "perfected" self is a temporary construct, always one life experience away from further transformation.

What if completion isn't an actual state but merely a conceptual framework we impose on the continuous flow of creation?

Botanist and Citizen Potawatomi Nation member Robin Wall Kimmerer offers an Indigenous perspective that naturally embraces the unfinished. Describing a basket weaver in "Braiding Sweetgrass," she observes: "The basket is not finished when the form is complete. It is finished when it has been given away" (Kimmerer, 2013).

This understanding views completion not as a final state but as a transition in relationship. The basket isn't an object to be perfected; it's a living connection between maker, materials, community, and future use. Its value lies not in reaching some endpoint, but in continuing its journey.

When we view our creative work through this lens, the anxiety about finishing transforms into appreciation for continuing. We recognize our creations are never truly "done"—they're always in conversation with the world, always part of an ongoing story that extends beyond our individual contribution.

The composer John Cage explored this idea through pieces like "4'33"---a work that consists of four minutes and thirty-three seconds of silence. The piece is never the same twice, as it's composed of the ambient sounds that occur while the musician sits without playing. It's never "complete" because it continues to be created in each performance through the unique sonic environment of that moment.

Cage's approach challenges the conventional understanding of what it means for a piece of music to be "finished." The work exists not as a fixed object but as an ongoing event---a framework for paying attention rather than a predetermined sequence of sounds.

This perspective isn't limited to experimental art. It applies to anything we create, whether symphonies or software, relationships or gardens, organizations or ideas. What we call "done" is simply a momentary snapshot of something that's continuously evolving.

Creation, by contrast, isn't a finish line but a state of being---a way of engaging with the world. It's dynamic, responsive, alive to possibility.

It doesn't seek to freeze reality into perfect forms but to participate in its ongoing unfolding.

The psychologist Mihaly Csikszentmihalyi, whose research on flow we explored earlier, found that people often experience the greatest fulfillment not in completion but in the creative process itself. The state of flow---of complete immersion in a challenging activity---provides more consistent joy than the moment of finishing.

This makes sense evolutionarily. If our satisfaction came primarily from completion, we would have little motivation to continue creating once basic survival needs were met. Instead, our brains reward the process of problem-solving, discovery, and creation itself---giving us dopamine not just for achieving goals but for the pursuit itself.

Some of the most meaningful aspects of life never reach completion at all. Relationships aren't projects to be finished but conversations that evolve over time. Spiritual practice isn't a course to be completed but an ongoing engagement with mystery. Parenting doesn't end with some final accomplishment but continues evolving through changing forms of connection.

To love something---whether a person, a practice, a calling---is to commit to its evolution. To engage not just with what it is now, but with what it's becoming. To participate in its unfolding rather than attempting to freeze it in perfect, completed form.

This perspective transforms how we approach our creative work, whatever form it takes. Rather than anxiously pushing toward completion, we can inhabit the creative state more fully. We can attend to what's emerging, respond to what's needed, and find joy in the engagement itself.

The Joy of Discontent

The poet Rainer Maria Rilke captured this beautifully in his advice to a young poet: "Be patient toward all that is unsolved in your heart and try to love the questions themselves... Do not now seek the answers, which cannot be given you because you would not be able to live them. And the point is, to live everything. Live the questions now."

Living the questions. Loving what's unsolved. Inhabiting the creative state rather than rushing toward completion. This is the invitation of the unfinished---to find joy not in being done, but in being fully engaged in the ongoing process of creation.

Story: The Lifelong Tinker

I once met a retired engineer who had a workshop full of half-finished inventions. Solar ovens. Adaptive crutches. Toy prototypes for kids with disabilities.

He'd never patented a thing.

He smiled and said, "I guess I'm more in love with the *trying* than the *completing.*"

And he meant it.

That room wasn't full of failures. It was full of *aliveness*. Curiosity. Attention. Care.

He was never "done," but he was deeply joyful.

Robert's workshop occupied a converted garage behind his modest home in the Midwest. From the outside, it looked unremarkable. Inside, it contained an extraordinary landscape of possibility---shelves lined with prototypes in various stages of development, walls covered with sketches and notes, tables bearing the organized chaos of ongoing projects.

Now in his late seventies, Robert had spent decades as a mechanical engineer for a large manufacturing company. His professional work had been solid and respected, if not particularly innovative. The company valued reliability over risk-taking, and Robert had delivered exactly that throughout his career.

But all the while, he had been building his own creative laboratory at home. Evenings and weekends, he would disappear into his workshop to pursue ideas that wouldn't leave him alone---inventions he believed could solve real problems, particularly for people with limited resources or physical disabilities.

"I grew up poor," he told me. "And I had a sister with cerebral palsy. I guess I never forgot what it feels like to need solutions that don't exist yet."

What struck me most about Robert's workshop wasn't just the creativity of the inventions---though many were genuinely clever---but his relationship to their unfinished state.

On one shelf sat a series of solar oven prototypes, each addressing limitations of the previous version. None was "perfect." Some had been abandoned when a new approach seemed more promising. Others were clearly still evolving.

"People ask why I don't finish them and take them to market," he said. "But for me, once the core problem is solved, my curiosity moves on. I'd rather work on the next challenge than spend years on manufacturing and marketing."

Another wall featured adjustable crutches designed for children in developing countries---made from locally available materials, easily repairable, and designed to "grow" with the child. Again, none had reached production.

"I send the designs to organizations that can use them," he explained. "Maybe someone will pick them up, maybe not. But the designs exist now. The possibility exists that wasn't there before."

What might look like a room full of abandoned projects was actually a space of continuous creation---a physical manifestation of ongoing curiosity and problem-solving. Robert didn't measure success by completion or commercialization. He measured it by engagement with meaningful questions.

When I asked if he regretted not bringing more inventions to market, his response revealed a profound contentment with the creative life he had chosen.

"I could have picked one thing and pushed it through---gotten patents, found investors, built a company. And then I'd have one finished product and a lot of business headaches," he laughed. "Instead, I've had fifty years of following my curiosity wherever it leads. I've solved dozens of interesting problems, even if only partially. For me, that's been the richer path."

Robert's approach challenges conventional measures of creative success. In a culture that celebrates the finished product, the measurable outcome, the monetizable innovation, his joy in the unfinished process itself represents a different kind of achievement.

His workshop wasn't full of failures. It was full of *aliveness*. Curiosity. Attention. Care. Each prototype represented not incompletion but authentic engagement with questions that mattered to him.

This perspective doesn't diminish the value of seeing things through to implementation. The world needs both the exploratory creators and those who transform possibilities into practicalities. But Robert's story reminds us that the unfinished isn't merely a waystation to completion. It's a valid creative state with its own particular joy.

He was never "done," but he was deeply joyful. And that joy came not despite the unfinished nature of his work, but because of his willingness to dwell in the creative middle---to value the process of discovery as much as the destination of completion.

BECOMING IS A LIFELONG STATE

There is no final version of you.

There is no endpoint where everything is sorted and settled.

And thank goodness.

To be human is to be in motion.

To keep learning, shifting, softening.

To say, again and again: *I'm still here. I'm still open. I'm still becoming.*

This is not resignation---it's relief.

It means we're not late. Not lost. Not broken.

Just in process.

Our culture harbors a peculiar fantasy: that somewhere in adulthood, we'll arrive at a finished version of ourselves. We'll finally have it figured out---our career, our relationships, our purpose, our peace. We'll reach a plateau where change becomes unnecessary because we've achieved some idealized state of completion.

This fantasy isn't just unrealistic---it fundamentally misunderstands what it means to be human.

Human development research increasingly shows that growth doesn't stop at some predetermined point. Throughout adulthood, our brains remain capable of forming new neural pathways. Our personalities continue to evolve. Our capacities for wisdom, compassion, and creative engagement can deepen well into old age.

As developmental psychologist Robert Kegan puts it, in essence, the development of the self is not the retaining of a fixed self but rather the evolution of the self. We are not meant to arrive at some final version but to continue becoming more complex, more integrated, more fully ourselves throughout life.

This ongoing evolution isn't a bug in the system. It's the system working exactly as designed.

Consider how this perspective transforms our relationship with life's challenges. When we believe in a finished self, every difficulty becomes an obstacle to arrival, a problem to overcome on the way to that idealized state. But when we embrace becoming as a lifelong process, challenges become opportunities for growth---not barriers to completion but doorways to the next evolution of who we are.

This shift in perspective brings tremendous relief. If there's no final version to achieve, we can stop measuring ourselves against an impossible standard. We can release the pressure to have it all figured out by some arbitrary deadline. We can stop feeling "behind" in the imaginary race to completion.

We are not static beings. We are processes in motion.

Chris LeBrón is 26. His career, like his music, is still becoming. He's a rising Dominican artist whose songs—sometimes raw, often reaching—carry the ache of someone still exploring, still stretching toward what matters. There's no polish for polish's sake. What he offers is in motion—unfolding with faith, curiosity, and heart. His path reminds us that we don't have to be finished to begin. Joy lives in the becoming.

This is why the metaphor of a "life's work" can be so misleading. It suggests a single, cohesive product—one grand achievement to cap a lifetime. But what if life isn't about producing a final work at all? What if it's about participating in a continuous process of creation and becoming?

We're not late. Not lost. Not broken. Just in process.

The Buddhist teacher Pema Chödrön captures this beautifully when she speaks of "abandoning hope" - not in the sense of despair, but in the sense of releasing attachment to fixed outcomes. Abandoning hope is an affirmation, the beginning of the beginning," she writes. "We can never know what will happen next.

This fundamental openness to continuing evolution lies at the heart of a meaningful life. Not the closed certainty of arrival, but the open possibility of becoming.

The poet Theodore Roethke expressed it this way: "I learn by going where I have to go." The learning and the going happen simultaneously. There is no point where the learning stops and the arrived self begins.

This perspective transforms not just how we view ourselves but how we relate to others. When we recognize that everyone is in a state of becoming, we can extend the same grace to others that we need for ourselves. We can see beyond current limitations to emerging possibilities. We can hold relationships as evolving conversations rather than fixed arrangements.

It also changes how we approach aging. Rather than seeing later life as a decline from some peak of development, we can recognize it as another phase of becoming---one with its own particular gifts, challenges, and opportunities for growth.

The Joy of Discontent

The psychologist James Hillman, in his book "The Force of Character," challenges the notion that youth represents the height of human development, with everything after being diminishment. Instead, he suggests that character continues to develop throughout life, with old age offering unique possibilities for wisdom, integration, and what he calls "ripening."

This ripening isn't about reaching completion. It's about continuing to engage with life's fundamental questions from an ever-deepening perspective. It's about becoming more fully who you are, not by finalizing some perfect version, but by remaining open to ongoing evolution.

There is no final version of you.

There is no endpoint where everything is sorted and settled.

And thank goodness.

To be human is to be in motion.

To keep learning, shifting, softening.

To say, again and again: *I'm still here. I'm still open. I'm still becoming.*

This is not resignation---it's relief.

Incompletion Isn't Inadequacy—

It's Invitation

What if the gaps in your story aren't things to fix, but places to play?

What if the things you haven't finished... are still speaking to you?

We often think of discontent as a flaw. But maybe it's just the echo of possibility---still bouncing through the spaces we've left open.

And maybe the most joyful way to live is to listen to that echo. To let it guide our hands, shape our days, soften our grip.

Our relationship with incompletion is deeply conflicted. On one hand, we're taught to finish what we start, to tie up loose ends, to achieve closure. On the other hand, we're surrounded by evidence that life itself is stubbornly, persistently unfinished---always in motion, always evolving, always revealing new dimensions.

This tension creates a particular kind of suffering. We feel inadequate because we haven't arrived at some imagined completion. Our unfinished projects, relationships, and self-development efforts seem to indict us---to suggest we lack the discipline, focus, or capability to reach the finish line.

But what if incompletion isn't evidence of inadequacy at all? What if it's actually an invitation - a doorway to continuing creativity, discovery, and growth?

The Japanese aesthetic tradition offers a profound reframe through the concept of *wabi-sabi* - the beauty of the imperfect, impermanent, and incomplete. Within this perspective, the unfinished isn't flawed; it's vibrant with possibility. The crack in the pot isn't a failure; it's where the light enters. The incomplete isn't lacking; it's alive.

This isn't just an aesthetic principle but a way of engaging with life itself. It suggests that the unresolved questions, the unfinished projects, the ongoing becoming---these aren't problems to solve but invitations to remain creatively engaged.

Consider your unfinished creative projects. Often we see these as failures---evidence of our inability to follow through. But what if they represent something else entirely? What if they are conversations we're still having with ourselves, questions we're still exploring, possibilities we're not yet ready to foreclose?

The Joy of Discontent

The writer Neil Gaiman illuminates this: "There's no such thing as a bad idea in the abstract—just ideas that haven't landed where they belong." The unfinished isn't flawed; it's still seeking its place.

Or think about relationships that feel unresolved. Our culture pushes for clean endings---clear breakups, formal closures, definitively finished chapters. But human connection rarely conforms to such tidy narratives. Relationships evolve, transform, sometimes lie dormant before reawakening in new forms. Their unfinished quality isn't necessarily a failure but a recognition of their living nature.

Even our understanding of ourselves remains gloriously incomplete. The unanswered questions about purpose, meaning, and identity aren't inadequacies to be overcome but ongoing conversations that keep us growing, discovering, and evolving throughout life.

This reframing of incompletion as invitation rather than inadequacy doesn't mean abandoning commitment or follow-through. Some things do benefit from completion. But it means holding a more spacious relationship with the unfinished parts of life---seeing them not as failures but as fertile ground for continuing growth.

The poet Rainer Maria Rilke advised: "Try to love the questions themselves, like locked rooms and like books that are written in a very foreign tongue." This love of the unresolved, the still-forming, the not-yet-known is at the heart of a creative relationship with incompletion.

We often think of discontent as a flaw. But maybe it's just the echo of possibility---still bouncing through the spaces we've left open. The twinge we feel when something remains unfinished isn't necessarily a problem. It might be life itself, asking for our continuing attention and care.

And maybe the most joyful way to live is to listen to that echo. To let it guide our hands, shape our days, soften our grip. Not to finish

The Beautiful Unfinished

everything, but to stay in conversation with what matters most---allowing life to remain a draft, a sketch, an ongoing creation rather than a completed work.

The invitation isn't to abandon care or commitment. It's to recognize that the most vital parts of life aren't about reaching some final state but about staying engaged with the process itself---about continuing to show up for the conversation, the creation, the becoming.

Incompletion isn't inadequacy---it's invitation. And accepting that invitation might be the most creative choice we can make.

A Practice: Bless the Unfinished

Take a moment to look around your life.

What is still in motion?

What have you not resolved?

What dreams, questions, or projects are quietly waiting---not for completion, but for your gentle attention?

Now bless them.

Not as failures. But as *companions*.

As signs that you are alive, that you still care, that you're not done being moved.

This practice invites a profound shift in how we relate to the unfinished dimensions of our lives. Rather than seeing them primarily as problems to solve or failures to overcome, we acknowledge them as vital aspects of an ongoing creative journey.

Begin by noticing. Look around your physical space, your calendar, your relationships, your inner landscape. Where do you find the unfinished? The projects started but not completed. The questions raised but not resolved. The relationships that remain complex rather than concluded. The aspects of yourself still in formation.

Make a gentle inventory---not to create another to-do list, but to bring awareness to the living, unresolved elements of your experience.

Then, instead of immediately strategizing how to finish or fix these elements, try something counterintuitive: bless them.

What does it mean to bless the unfinished? It means to recognize its value. To appreciate what it offers. To see it not as lacking but as fertile with possibility.

You might literally speak a blessing over these unfinished elements: "I bless this unfinished manuscript for what it has taught me about patience." "I bless this ongoing question about my purpose for keeping me engaged with what matters." "I bless this evolving relationship for its continuing invitation to growth."

Or you might simply sit with each unfinished element, acknowledging its place in your life with kindness rather than frustration. Notice what happens when you shift from seeing incompletion as a problem to recognizing it as a sign of ongoing engagement.

This blessing doesn't mean you'll never complete anything. Some projects do benefit from conclusion. Some questions do find satisfying, if temporary, answers. But the blessing changes your relationship with the unfinished---from one of anxiety or inadequacy to one of appreciation for the continuing conversation.

The unfinished aspects of your life aren't failures of discipline or signs of inadequacy. They're companions on the journey. They're evidence that you're still engaged, still curious, still open to becoming.

They show that you're alive. That you still care. That you're not done being moved.

And there's a particular joy in this recognition---not the satisfied relief of completion, but the deeper joy of ongoing vitality. Of continuing to care, to question, to create, to become.

This practice doesn't ask you to remain permanently unfinished in every area. Some completion is valuable and necessary. But it invites you to hold a more spacious relationship with incompletion---to see it not merely as absence of ending but as presence of continuing possibility.

As the poet Mary Oliver writes: "Things take the time they take. Don't worry. How many roads did St. Augustine follow before he became St. Augustine?" The unfinished isn't failed; it's still becoming. And blessing it acknowledges the value in that ongoing process.

Live Like the Ending Doesn't Matter

You are allowed to write without knowing the last chapter.

To build what no one asked for.

To love what may never be returned.

To wake up every day and still say: *Yes, I will try again.*

That is courage.

That is grace.

That is the joy of the beautiful unfinished.

Our cultural narratives are saturated with endings. The hero's journey concludes with triumphant return. The romance ends in wedding or heartbreak. The business journey culminates in acquisition or bankruptcy. The spiritual quest reaches enlightenment or despair.

These narrative patterns shape how we understand our own lives, encouraging us to orient toward definitive outcomes---to measure the journey's value by its ending.

But what if the ending doesn't matter as much as we think? What if the meaning isn't primarily in how things conclude, but in how fully we engage with each step along the way?

Living like the ending doesn't matter isn't about indifference to outcomes. It's about refusing to let those outcomes determine the value of the process itself. It's about recognizing that meaning exists in the engagement, not just in the conclusion.

The writer Anne Lamott touches on this when she describes why she writes—she tells the truth in service to life and uses writing to discover what she thinks, who she is, and what she believes. For Lamott, writing isn't merely a means to produce a finished book. It's a way of engaging with life itself—a process valuable regardless of its outcome.

This perspective applies far beyond writing. Entrepreneurs start businesses not just to achieve particular financial outcomes, but because they value the creative process of building something. Scientists pursue research not just for definitive answers, but for the joy of inquiry itself. Parents raise children not as projects to be completed, but as relationships to be engaged with over time.

In each case, there's a willingness to value the journey independently of its conclusion---to find meaning in the engagement itself rather than deferring meaning to some future outcome.

This doesn't mean abandoning care about results. It means recognizing that results are only one dimension of meaning, and often not the most important one. It means valuing process at least as much as product, becoming at least as much as arrival.

The theologian and philosopher Howard Thurman captured this when he said: "Don't ask yourself what the world needs. Ask yourself what makes you come alive, and go do that, because what the world needs is people who have come alive."

Coming alive isn't about reaching endpoints. It's about engaging fully with what matters -about bringing your whole self to each moment of creation, connection, and becoming. It's about valuing aliveness itself, not just what that aliveness produces.

This perspective transforms how we approach creative work. We create not just to finish or to achieve external validation, but because the act of creation itself is meaningful. We follow curiosity not just to arrive at answers, but because curiosity itself enriches our experience. We build relationships not just to reach particular outcomes, but because connection itself holds value.

Living like the ending doesn't matter frees us from the paralysis of uncertainty. If we need to know how things will turn out before we begin, we severely limit what we're willing to attempt. But if we value the engagement itself, we can step into uncertainty with greater courage and openness.

You are allowed to write without knowing the last chapter.

To build what no one asked for.

To love what may never be returned.

To wake up every day and still say: *Yes, I will try again.*

This willingness to engage without guarantees isn't recklessness. It's a recognition that life itself is unfinished---that we never have complete certainty about outcomes, that every ending is also a beginning, that meaning exists in the living itself rather than in some final conclusion.

The poet Rainer Maria Rilke wrote: "Be patient toward all that is unsolved in your heart and try to love the questions themselves, like locked rooms and like books that are written in a very foreign tongue."

Loving the questions. Embracing the unresolved. Finding joy in the beautiful unfinished. This isn't settling for less; it's recognizing the richness that exists in the ongoing process of creation and becoming.

That is courage.

That is grace.

That is the joy of the beautiful unfinished.

Reflection: Honoring Your Unfinished Symphony

Consider these questions as invitations rather than assignments. There are no right answers---only your honest reflection.

1. What unfinished aspects of your life have you been treating as problems rather than possibilities?
2. Where have you been postponing joy until after some imagined completion? What might change if you allowed joy in the unfinished present?
3. What would it look like to value becoming over arrival in your creative work? In your relationships? In your self-development?
4. How might your relationship with discontent shift if you saw it not as a flaw but as a sign of continuing engagement with what matters?
5. What unfinished project or question continues to call to you? What might it be asking for---not necessarily completion, but perhaps renewed attention?

The Beautiful Unfinished

Remember that these reflections aren't meant to add to your to-do list or create new pressures for completion. They're invitations to explore a different relationship with the unfinished---one based in appreciation rather than anxiety, in curiosity rather than criticism.

The unfinished isn't failed. It's alive. And that aliveness deserves not just acknowledgment but celebration.

Your unfinished symphony isn't waiting for a perfect conclusion. It's playing now, note by note, through the everyday improvisations of your life. Listen. Engage. Play your part.

Maybe we were never meant to arrive. Maybe we were only ever meant to *engage*. To create. To care. In this final reflection, let's return to that truth---and leave space for what's still becoming in you.

The joy is in the music itself.

The Joy of Discontent

CHAPTER 7

In Practice — Honoring What Stirs

> **Threshold**
> What stirs in you, stirs the world.
> Not a burden to silence,
> but a voice to honor.
> Let it speak.
> Let it move.
> Let it become.

*T*his chapter is not an ending. It is a threshold. An open invitation to walk forward with what's been stirred.

The pages you've read are not meant to be mastered. They're meant to be returned to. Lingered with. Marked up. Forgotten, then rediscovered. This book is not a ladder. It is a field. A fire. A quiet breath beside you when everything else gets loud.

You've walked through ache, friction, stillness, rebellion, and unfinishedness. You've sat with questions that don't resolve and truths that don't demand perfection. That in itself is sacred.

A Creative Companion

What follows are invitations to stay in creative relationship with your discontent—not as homework, but as heartwork. You'll find chapter-specific reflections and enduring practices to return to, again and again. Take what serves you. Leave what doesn't. Let your instincts guide your becoming.

Each chapter explored a different dimension of creative discontent. Here are practices to deepen your relationship with each.

From Chapter 1 — The Myth of Arrival

- **Timeline Reversal:** Draw your life not as a progress toward endpoints, but as a series of engagements. What changes when you see your journey this way?
- **Arrival Audit:** What are you currently postponing until "after" something is achieved? ("I'll rest after this project." "I'll be present after this milestone.") Choose one thing you're postponing and bring a small version of it into the present.
- **The Middle Practice:** For one day, consciously frame every activity as a middle—not working toward completion but engaging with process. Notice how this shift affects your experience.
- **Letter to Discontent:** Write a letter to your discontent. Let it speak back. What is it trying to tell you that you might not want to hear?
- **Success Redefined:** Create your own definition of success that centers alignment rather than arrival. What would your days look like if you measured by engagement rather than achievement?

In Practice — Honoring What Stirs

From Chapter 2 — Restlessness as a Creative Compass

- **Compass Check:** When have you felt restless in a way that wasn't destructive, but clarifying? What did that restlessness lead you toward?
- **The Twitch Follow:** Each day for a week, notice one thing that catches your attention—something that creates a small "twitch" of interest. Follow it for five minutes, even if it seems impractical or unimportant.
- **Restlessness Mapping:** Draw a map of where restlessness lives in your body. When you feel that creative tension, where do you physically experience it? Getting to know its texture and location can help you recognize it as a familiar messenger rather than an intrusion.
- **The Care Question:** Ask yourself: "What do I care about so much that I'm willing to feel uncomfortable for it?" This question reveals where your creative restlessness connects to deeper values.
- **Curiosity Trail:** Choose something you encounter regularly but have never really explored—a plant on your walking route, the history of your neighborhood, how something in your home actually works. Follow your curiosity about this ordinary thing and see where it leads.

From Chapter 3 — The Friction That Fuels Flow

- **Threshold Inventory:** Identify three activities where you regularly experience resistance before flow. Write down the specific qualities of the resistance—what thoughts, feelings, or sensations signal you're at the threshold?
- **Flow Audit:** When do you feel most alive? Track moments of flow for a week. Note what you were doing, the conditions that supported it, and how you moved through initial resistance.

- **Five More Minutes:** When you feel the urge to abandon a challenging creative task, commit to five more minutes. Often this is enough to move through the threshold resistance into deeper engagement.
- **Ritual Design:** Create a simple ritual that signals to your mind and body that you're entering creative space. It might be lighting a candle, arranging your materials in a specific way, or taking three deep breaths. Use this ritual consistently to build a neural pathway to focused engagement.
- **Friction Reframe:** Next time you encounter creative resistance, try saying: "This is the threshold. This is normal. This means I'm getting close to something that matters." Notice how this reframe affects your relationship with the resistance.

From Chapter 4 — Creating Without Clinging

- **The Offering Practice:** Make something today and deliberately release any attachment to how it's received. Create it, complete it, and consider it an offering rather than an achievement.
- **Private Creation:** Commit to a small creative project that you will never share. Notice how the absence of potential audience affects your creative process and experience.
- **The Letting Go Ritual:** Choose something you've created that you've been holding tightly—seeking validation, worrying about reception, trying to perfect. Create a small ritual to symbolically release your grip on it. This might be as simple as writing down your anxieties about it and then tearing up the paper.
- **Process Documentation:** For one creative session, document your process rather than focusing solely on the outcome.

Take photos at different stages, write notes about your decision-making, capture the evolution. This shifts attention from product to process.
- **The Freedom Question:** Before beginning a creative project, ask: "What would I create if I didn't need it to be impressive?" Let the answer guide your next steps.

From Chapter 5 — Joy as Rebellion

- **Beauty Census:** In a space you consider broken, neglected, or problematic, deliberately look for evidence of beauty, care, or resistance. Document what you find—the plant growing through concrete, the graffiti that speaks truth, the unexpected kindness.
- **Joy Cartography:** Map where joy and discontent intersect in your life. Where is your joy pushing back against numbness? Where does your discontent fuel creative action rather than despair?
- **The Small Rebellion:** Name one small, subversive act of care you can offer your world. Something that says, "Things could be different." Then do it.
- **Rebel Ancestors:** Research someone who used creativity as resistance in a context similar to yours—whether in art, teaching, business, parenting, or community work. What can you learn from their approach?
- **The Ask:** What remains unacceptable to you? What can't you make peace with? What spark of rebellion still burns? Let yourself feel the full strength of this discontent, then ask: "What creative response might I offer?"

From Chapter 6 — The Beautiful Unfinished

- **The Gallery of Unfinished:** Create a small display of unfinished projects, drafts, or ideas. Instead of seeing them as failures, honor them as evidence of your continuing creativity and curiosity.
- **The Now Practice:** For one day, practice speaking without using future or past tenses. Like the Pirahã, try staying in immediate experience. Notice how this affects your sense of completeness or incompleteness.
- **Blessing the Unfinished:** Identify something incomplete in your life right now. Instead of seeing it as a problem, offer it a blessing: "I bless this unfinished [project/question/relationship] for what it continues to teach me."
- **Present Sufficiency:** Complete this sentence: "Even without finishing [something important to you], I am still..." Let this reminder of your inherent value beyond accomplishment sink in.
- **Wabi-Sabi Observation:** Find something in your environment that embodies wabi-sabi—the beauty of the imperfect, impermanent, and incomplete. A weathered fence, a chipped mug you love, a garden in transition. Spend five minutes in quiet observation of its particular beauty.

PRACTICES TO RETURN TO

These ongoing practices can be touchstones on your journey—ways to stay in conversation with your creative discontent across contexts and challenges.

The Gentle Question

When tension rises, when restlessness stirs, when creative discontent makes itself known, pause. Take a breath. And ask with genuine curiosity: "What is stirring in me? What might it be asking for?"

This isn't a question that needs an immediate answer. It's an invitation to relationship—to treating your discontent not as a problem to solve but as a messenger to hear. Sometimes the answer will come immediately. Sometimes it will emerge over days or weeks. Sometimes it will reveal itself only through creative action.

The practice is not in finding the perfect answer, but in continuing to ask with openness rather than judgment.

The Joy Map

Once a month, take time to map your recent moments of deep joy and engagement—especially those that began in discomfort or discontent. Where did you feel most alive? Most present? Most in flow? What conditions surrounded these experiences? What initial resistance did you move through?

Over time, these maps become a personal atlas of your creative landscape—showing the territories where your discontent most often transforms into joy, where your restlessness leads to meaningful engagement, where your friction ignites flow.

Use this evolving understanding not as rigid rules, but as helpful guidance when you feel lost or stuck.

The Creative Sabbath

In many spiritual traditions, sabbath represents not just rest, but sacred time—set apart from productivity, achievement, and utility. Consider establishing a regular "Creative Sabbath"—time dedicated to creation for its own sake, free from any expectation of outcome or use.

This might be an hour each week, a day each month, or any rhythm that fits your life. The only requirement is that what you create during this time is "useless" by conventional standards—made purely for the joy of making, for the conversation with materials, for the engagement with process.

Protect this time from the incursion of practical concerns. Call it sacred. Because it is.

The Sacred No

Discernment is essential to creative living. Not everything that calls for your attention deserves your engagement. The "Sacred No" is a practice of intentional release—not as failure or abandonment, but as conscious choice.

Regularly reflect on what you're carrying that no longer serves your deepest creative calling. What projects, commitments, or expectations can you release with intention? What "good ideas" need to be composted to make room for what truly matters now?

The Sacred No isn't rejection. It's reallocation of your finite creative energy toward what most deeply calls you.

The Twitch Tracker

The "twitch" is that subtle internal movement—a flicker of interest, a question that won't leave you alone, a spark of curiosity or concern that catches your attention. These twitches are creative clues, pointing toward what matters to you, what needs your attention, what might want to emerge through you.

In Practice — Honoring What Stirs

Keep a simple log of these twitches when they arise. Not to immediately act on all of them, but to develop greater awareness of your creative stirrings. Over time, patterns emerge—showing the questions, concerns, and possibilities that consistently call to you.

This awareness becomes a compass, helping you recognize the difference between random distraction and genuine creative calling.

The Body Check

Discontent, restlessness, creative tension—these aren't just mental states. They live in the body. The Body Check is a simple practice of pausing to notice the physical sensations of your creative state.

Where do you feel restlessness in your body? How does creative excitement manifest physically? What sensations accompany creative blockage or resistance? Where do you feel the satisfaction of meaningful engagement?

This somatic awareness helps you recognize your creative states more quickly and respond more appropriately—distinguishing between the resistance that precedes flow, the restlessness that signals misalignment, and the tension that indicates creative possibility.

The Threshold Reminder

Create a physical reminder of the threshold principle—that the resistance before flow is not an obstacle but a doorway. This might be a small stone you keep where you work, a symbol drawn on your notebook, or a word or phrase posted where you'll see it.

When you encounter creative resistance, touch this reminder. Let it ground you in the knowledge that what you're experiencing isn't failure or inadequacy. It's the threshold—the place where engagement deepens if you're willing to stay.

The Joy of Discontent

A Final Reflection— Stay Restless, Stay True

And yet, even in the act of practice, something deeper stirs.
Beyond what we do lies who we're becoming.
For the Ones Still Becoming
To the ones who begin again,
who let the ache stay open,
who plant without knowing
what will bloom—
this world was made
for you.

You've made it to the end of this book.

But I hope, in some way, it doesn't feel like an ending at all.

If anything, I hope it feels like a return—

to the part of you that was never trying to arrive.

The part that already knew: joy doesn't come from being complete.

It comes from being *awake*.

You've read stories of restlessness, friction, flow, rebellion, and the beautiful unfinished.

Not as abstract ideas, but as companions on the creative path.

As mirrors to your own experience.

Because you, too, have felt it—the tension, the pull, the quiet hum that says,

There's something here worth caring about.

That is discontent.

Not the bitter kind, but the kind that breathes.

That notices.

That creates.

You Are Not Behind

If you are still figuring it out,

if you are still scribbling, tinkering, revising, rebuilding—

good.

It means you are still *in it*.

It means you're engaged.

It means you haven't let the world numb you into stillness.

You are not behind.

You are on the path.

And the path is not straight. It is not clear.

But it is alive.

And it is yours.

Our culture bombards us with timelines—for career advancement, creative achievement, relationship milestones, financial stability. We internalize these schedules, these ladders of progress, until they become the measuring sticks against which we judge our lives.

But these timelines are largely artificial constructs. They reflect neither the complex reality of human development nor the unique rhythms of individual lives. They impose linear expectations on non-linear journeys.

When we measure ourselves against these arbitrary timelines, we often come to the painful conclusion that we're "behind"—that we should be further along, more accomplished, more settled, more certain than we currently are.

This sense of being behind creates a particular kind of suffering. It transforms the present moment from a place of potential into a place of lack. It reframes our ongoing becoming as inadequacy rather than aliveness.

But what if the timeline itself is the problem? What if the very notion of being "behind" misunderstands how growth, creativity, and meaningful living actually unfold?

Creative work—whether making art, building relationships, crafting a career, or shaping a life—rarely follows predictable timelines. It moves at the speed of discovery, which can't be scheduled or standardized. It includes fallow periods that appear unproductive but are essential for integration and renewal. It responds to intuitive pulls that don't align with external expectations.

As the poet Mary Oliver writes, "Things take the time they take. Don't worry. How many roads did St. Augustine follow before he became St. Augustine?"

The most meaningful paths are rarely the most direct. They include wanderings, explorations, apparent detours that later reveal themselves as essential. They involve periods of uncertainty that eventually yield deeper clarity. They require seasons of questioning that make later conviction more authentic.

You are not behind.

You are exactly where your particular journey has brought you.

And that place—with all its questions, uncertainties, and unfinished elements—is not a waiting room for your real life. It is your real life, unfolding in real time.

The invitation isn't to catch up to some imagined schedule. It's to fully inhabit the path you're actually on—to engage with the questions that matter to you, to follow the creative pulls that enliven you, to remain responsive to your own evolving sense of meaning and purpose.

This doesn't mean abandoning all structure or direction. It means holding any plans or timelines as flexible frameworks rather than rigid requirements. It means valuing your actual growth process, with all its messy non-linearity, over idealized, predictable progress.

If you are still figuring it out—still experimenting, still questioning, still refining your understanding of yourself and your work—that's not failure or delay. It's engagement. It's aliveness. It's the courage to remain in the creative middle rather than rushing to premature conclusions.

The alternative isn't faster progress. It's numbness. It's disconnection from your own authentic becoming. It's settling for what's expected rather than exploring what's possible.

So release the timeline. Release the comparison. Release the arbitrary standards of where you "should" be by now.

You are not behind.

You are on the path.

And the path is not straight. It is not clear.

But it is alive.

And it is yours.

Stay Restless

When discontent shows up again—and it will—don't rush to fix it.

Sit with it.

Listen.

The Joy of Discontent

Ask:

- What is this trying to teach me?
- Where am I being invited to grow, to soften, to stretch?
- What wants to be made through me next?

Stay with the questions.

Let them stir something.

Let them move you, even slightly.

We've explored throughout this book how creative discontent serves as an internal compass—pointing toward what matters, what's misaligned, what wants to emerge. This restlessness isn't a problem to solve but a signal to honor—a vital communication from the part of you that remains engaged with life's possibilities.

Yet our instinct, conditioned by a culture that prizes comfort and certainty, is often to silence this signal. To treat discontent as a glitch rather than guidance. To fix it, numb it, or rush past it toward false resolution.

The invitation here is different: stay restless.

This doesn't mean clinging to dissatisfaction or cultivating chronic unhappiness. It means maintaining your capacity to be moved—to notice when something doesn't feel right, to sense when more is possible, to respond to the subtle urgings toward greater alignment, authenticity, and aliveness.

Staying restless means refusing the trance of completion—the illusion that you will someday arrive at a finished state where growth stops and certainty reigns. It means recognizing that the most meaningful life isn't one that reaches some imagined destination, but one that remains responsive to ongoing calls for creation, connection, and becoming.

In Practice — Honoring What Stirs

When discontent arises, rather than immediately trying to resolve it, create space to listen to what it might be telling you. Is it pointing toward misalignment between your actions and your values? Is it revealing an area where you've been playing too small? Is it highlighting a genuine need for rest or recalibration? Is it inviting you toward new creative territory?

The questions themselves matter more than immediate answers. They create a container for the discontent—not to eliminate it, but to engage with it as a source of potential insight and direction.

This engagement transforms how you experience restlessness. Rather than resisting it as unwelcome discomfort, you can welcome it as a familiar companion on the creative journey—one that keeps you honest, keeps you moving, keeps you engaged with what matters most.

The journalist and activist Ta-Nehisi Coates captures this relationship with restlessness when he describes his writing process: "I always consider the entire process about failure, and I think that's the reason why I keep going." For Coates, the sense of not-quite-rightness, of not-yet-there, isn't an obstacle to creativity but its very engine.

The same can be true in any domain. The teacher who maintains creative restlessness continues evolving their approach rather than settling into comfortable routine. The relationship that honors creative restlessness remains vital rather than calcifying into habit. The organization that values creative restlessness stays responsive to emerging needs rather than clinging to outdated methods.

Staying restless doesn't mean constant disruption or perpetual dissatisfaction. It means maintaining a dynamic relationship with your own becoming—a willingness to keep asking questions, to keep noticing what feels misaligned, to keep responding to life's invitations for growth and creation.

It means trusting that the discomfort of not knowing, not arriving, not being finished isn't a problem. It's the feeling of being fully alive to your own potential.

So when discontent shows up—when you feel that familiar stirring, that sense that something isn't quite right or something more is possible—don't rush to silence it. Don't treat it as evidence of failure or weakness.

Stay with it. Listen to it. Ask what it might be trying to tell you.

Let it be not the end of something, but the beginning.

Stay True

Stay true to what lights you up, even if it doesn't make sense to anyone else.

Stay true to your curiosity, your care, your creative ache.

Let it guide you—not to a perfect life, but to a present one.

A life of motion, attention, and quiet rebellion.

The joy of discontent is not about having the answers.

It's about staying in the dance.

In a world that often pressures us toward conformity, staying true to your own creative path requires a particular kind of courage. It means honoring your unique curiosity, following your distinctive pulls, making choices that align with your internal compass rather than external expectations.

This isn't about blind self-indulgence or disregard for others. It's about recognizing that your specific combination of interests, values,

In Practice — Honoring What Stirs

questions, and creative tensions isn't random or insignificant. It's a compass pointing toward your unique contribution.

When you feel lit up by something—a question, a possibility, a creative direction—that enthusiasm isn't trivial. It's information. It's guidance about where your energy wants to flow, where your attention naturally focuses, where you might make your most meaningful contribution.

This guidance often doesn't match external expectations or conventional paths. It might lead you toward hybrid careers that don't fit neatly into job descriptions. Toward creative projects that cross traditional boundaries. Toward ways of living that prioritize values different from those dominant in your culture.

Staying true to this internal guidance doesn't guarantee ease or external validation. It often means moving against the current, making choices others don't understand, facing questions about practicality or security or conformity.

But it offers something more valuable than easy approval: the deep satisfaction of living in alignment with your own authenticity. The joy of engaging with what genuinely matters to you. The aliveness that comes from following your actual path rather than someone else's prescription.

The poet Mary Oliver captures this perfectly in her famous question: "Tell me, what is it you plan to do with your one wild and precious life?" The emphasis on "your" is crucial. Not the life others expect of you. Not the life that would look most impressive on paper. But your life—the one that aligns with your particular constellation of passions, values, and creative tensions.

Staying true doesn't mean having perfect clarity or unwavering certainty. It means remaining in conversation with your own evolving sense of meaning and purpose. It means noticing when you've drifted into choices based primarily on others' expectations, and gently redirecting toward what genuinely matters to you.

This ongoing alignment requires regular reflection. What activities bring you a sense of flow and engagement? Where do you lose track of time? What topics or questions do you find yourself returning to, even when no one else seems interested? What values feel non-negotiable, even when prioritizing them comes at a cost?

The answers to these questions offer clues to your authentic path—not a predetermined destination, but a direction that honors who you are and what you care about most deeply.

Following this path rarely leads to perfection. It leads to presence—to being fully engaged with your actual life rather than constantly straining toward some idealized version. It leads to a life characterized not by flawless execution but by genuine care, curious attention, and honest expression.

The joy of discontent is not about having the answers.

It's about staying in the dance.

It's about remaining engaged with the questions that matter to you, responsive to the creative tensions that enliven you, committed to the values that define you—even when that engagement isn't easy or immediately rewarded.

This kind of authentic engagement doesn't eliminate difficulty or guarantee specific outcomes. But it offers something perhaps more valuable: the profound satisfaction of living your actual life rather than someone else's version of it. The joy of creating not what the world expects, but what only you can offer.

Stay true to what lights you up, even if it doesn't make sense to anyone else.

In Practice — Honoring What Stirs

Stay true to your curiosity, your care, your creative ache.

Let it guide you—not to a perfect life, but to a present one.

A life of motion, attention, and quiet rebellion.

The River and the Stones

Imagine a river—not the powerful rush of white water, but a quieter current that moves steadily through a landscape. The river doesn't arrive. It flows. It doesn't finish its journey; it is the journey. Its nature is movement, not arrival.

Along its banks are smooth stones. Each one was once jagged, irregular, full of edges. But the river—in its patient, persistent motion—has transformed them. Not by force, but by relationship. Not in a day, but over time. The river didn't set out to perfect the stones. It simply flowed, and in that flowing, the stones were changed.

You are both the river and the stone.

You are the flowing—the creative current that moves through your days, that shapes and reshapes what it touches. And you are the being shaped—the self that is smoothed and polished not by violent change but by consistent engagement with what matters.

The joy isn't in reaching some final state of perfection. It's in the flowing itself. In the relationship between what moves through you and what is moved by you. In the dance between changing and being changed.

Look at your hands. They hold the capacity to shape something that wasn't there before. To make visible what exists only in your mind's eye. To bring forth what the world hasn't yet imagined it needs.

So as you close this book and continue your journey, carry this image with you: You are the river and the stone. Always flowing, always being shaped, never finished, always becoming.

The Joy of Discontent

One Last Whisper

You don't have to be finished.
You don't have to be certain.
You don't have to wait.
You just have to begin.
And then begin again.

Because you are allowed to be a work in progress.

And that, too, is beautiful.

The world doesn't need more people who have it all figured out. It needs people who remain curious, caring, and creative in the face of complexity. People who aren't afraid of questions or challenges or the beautiful unfinished. People who bring their full humanity to each moment of their lives.

It needs you—not some perfect, polished, completed version of you. But you as you are right now, with all your questions and cares and creative tensions. You with your particular discontent, your distinctive vision, your unique capacity to notice what others might miss and create what others might never imagine.

This is not a blank page for you to become something different. It is a mirror for you to see what's already there. The unfinished symphony that is you— playing its next note.

What creative current is flowing through you right now, waiting to shape the world?

Stay restless.

Stay true.

The becoming continues.

Acknowledgments

This book began with a whisper—a discomfort I couldn't ignore. But it was a twitch that made me move. That small, embodied nudge has grown into something bigger, which I explore more fully in my next project: *Flip the TWITCH*.

Along the way, I've been shaped by a constellation of thinkers, teachers, and companions— most I've met only through the intimacy of their work.

To Mihaly Csikszentmihalyi, whose exploration of flow opened the doorway to understanding presence, purpose, and the paradox of joy within effort.

To Todd Kashdan, for showing that discomfort can be a source of insight, and that curiosity is not only a trait, but a way of walking through the world.

To Daniel Everett, whose bold study of the Pirahã challenged conventional thinking about language, time, and cultural assumptions—inviting us to imagine what a truly present-tense life might feel like.

To Octavia Butler, whose concept of "positive obsession" gave name to the persistent creative restlessness that propels meaningful work.

To bell hooks, for illuminating how love and care can be forms of quiet rebellion in a detached world.

To Robin Wall Kimmerer, whose integration of Indigenous wisdom and scientific knowledge offers a model for embracing the beautiful unfinished.

To Bayo Akomolafe, whose invitation to "slow down" in urgent times reminds us that meaning emerges in the spaces between action.

To Margaret Wheatley, who continues to hold space for deep listening, human-centered leadership, and the dignity of emergence in complex systems.

To David Bohm, whose work on dialogue, wholeness, and the implicate order continues to ripple through my thinking. His belief in unfolding meaning echoes quietly throughout these pages.

To David Whyte, Ursula K. Le Guin, Mary Oliver, Parker Palmer, and adrienne maree brown, whose poetic clarity and moral imagination have helped me remember what matters most.

And to the quiet creators—the unseen teachers, artists, builders, caregivers, and wanderers—who feel the hum of something more. This book is for you.

Suggested Reading & Inspirations

If parts of this book stirred something in you, these voices may deepen that resonance. Each helped shape the creative and philosophical ground on which *The Joy of Discontent* stands.

- **Flow** – Mihaly Csikszentmihalyi
- **The Art of Insubordination** – Todd Kashdan
- **Don't Sleep, There Are Snakes** – Daniel Everett
- **Turning to One Another** – Margaret Wheatley
- **Braiding Sweetgrass** - Robin Wall Kimmerer
- **All About Love** - bell hooks
- **Bloodchild and Other Stories** -- Octavia Butler
- **These Wilds Beyond Our Fences** - Bayo Akomolafe
- **Wholeness and the Implicate Order** - David Bohm
- **Crossing the Unknown Sea** - David Whyte
- **The Dispossessed** - Ursula K. Le Guin
- **Devotions** - Mary Oliver
- **Emergent Strategy** - adrienne maree brown
- **Let Your Life Speak** - Parker J. Palmer

These aren't required readings. They're companions—lights along the path of creative becoming.

About the Author

David S. Morgan is a bold, curious thinker who lives at the intersection of creativity, innovation, and human potential. With over three decades of experience as an inventor, CEO, and change agent, he has led transformative efforts across sectors—helping people and organizations grow, adapt, and reimagine what's possible in times of disruption.

David's work explores the tension between structure and soul, systems and story, discontent and becoming. Whether writing about artificial intelligence or the creative spirit, he is known for blending strategic insight with emotional depth—offering readers both clarity and invitation.

The Joy of Discontent is his most personal book yet—a soulful guide to honoring restlessness as a creative force and companion in the journey of becoming.

When he's not writing, speaking, or challenging the status quo, you'll likely find him exploring the woods of New Hampshire, sketching out ideas on paper napkins, or getting lost in the questions that won't let him go.

He welcomes thoughtful dialogue and collaboration. You can reach him at **davidceonh@gmail.com**.

Other Books by David S. Morgan

- **AI-PROOF MANIFESTO:** *The New Rules of Work in the Age of Intelligent Machines and the Seven Superpowers to Rewrite Your Rules*
- **Generation Innovate:** *Unleashing the Creative Revolution of Millennials and Gen-Z*
- **GOALS:** *The Ultimate Guide to Personal and Team Triumph*
- **Ten Steps to Innovating Your Nonprofit:** *How to Build a Dynamic, Creative, Innovative Nonprofit*

Notes

www.ingramcontent.com/pod-product-compliance
Lightning Source LLC
LaVergne TN
LVHW041336080426
835512LV00006B/492